Women and elderly on the BSR labour market - good practices' analysis and transfer

Authors
Marzena Grzesiak Ph.D. (Part I 2, Part II, Part III 2)
Magdalena Olczyk Ph.D. (Foreword, Part I 1, Part III 1)
Anita Richert-Kaźmierska Ph.D. (Part I 2, Part II, Part III 2)
Marzena Starnawska Ph.D. (Part I 1, Part III 1, Summary)

All articles in this publication are scientifically reviewed by members of the editorial board.

Published by
Baltic Sea Academy e.V.
Dr Max Hogefoster
Blankeneser Landstrasse, 22587 Hamburg, Germany

Editorial Correspondence: editor@baltic-sea-academy.eu;

Manufactured and published by BoD-Books on Demand, Norderstedt, Germany
© 2014 Baltic Sea Academy e.V. All rights reserved.

ISBN 9783735791412

Part-financed by the European Union (European Development Fund and European Neighbourhood and Partnership Instrument) within BSR QUICK IGA project. This publication does not necessarily reflect the opinion of the European Commision.

We are very grateful to the European Commision for the financial support and also to the Joint Technical Secretariat of the INTERREG IVB Programme for the support and advice.

Content

Foreword

The idea for this book was born in year 2012 as an aftermath of global discussion in the press and television on the long-term strategy for European Union growth and development. Published on March 3, 2010 EC's Statement "Europe 2020 - A strategy for smart, sustainable and inclusive growth" emphasized the need for joint action by Member States to overcome the crisis and the implementation of reforms for tackling the challenges of globalization, aging populations or the increasing need for rational use of resource. In order to achieve these objectives three basic, mutually reinforcing priorities were proposed: smart growth, i.e. the development based on knowledge and innovation, sustainable growth, which is the transition towards a low carbon, resource efficient and competitive economy and inclusive growth, which supports economy characterized by a high-employment , social and territorial cohesion.

According to the authors, in long-term horizon the biggest challenge facing the European Union is the increase of population activity on the European labor market. Achieving the objective enclosed in the Europe 2020 Strategy, i.e. the employment rate of people aged 20-64 should reach 75%, may be achieved only by increasing the activity of women and the elderly [Strategy 2020]. And those two groups of people have become of interest to the authors.

Analysis of macroeconomic data carried out by the authors indicated that the employment rate among women and older people in Scandinavian countries such as Denmark, Sweden, Norway is much higher than in other EU countries [Eurostat, 2012]. Thus the idea was born to identify and transfer of best practices from the Northern European countries to selected countries of the Baltic Sea Region (Poland Germany, Lithuania and Latvia). The choice of countries to which best practices should be transferred, was the result of the authors' participation in IGA "Innovative SMEs by Gender and Age" initiative. This project is a partnership including 13 partners from 7 BSR countries, which have specific experiences in SME promotion in the field of innovation and gender equality. 3 partners from Finland, Sweden and Norway deliver best practices, 10 partners from 4 southern BSR countries develop, test and implement these practices. Part of the analyzes presented in this book has been prepared as the internal QUICK IGA project's reports: *The best practices transfer part I* [Grzesiak, Olczyk, Starnawska 2013], *The best practices transfer part II* [Grzesiak, Olczyk, Richert-Kaźmierska, Starnawska 2013] and *The analysis of the conditions for best practices' transfer* [Grzesiak, Richert-Kaźmierska 2013]. To make the results of analysis, good practices descriptions and recommendations of transfer's conditions more widely available, authors decided to publish that material in the form of this book.

This book was designed to differ from other books available on the market and dealing with activation of women and older people in the European labour market. Already the combined analysis of these two groups in one study constitutes a novelty. However, the authors focused on the one hand on the complex, and on the other hand, on a practical approach to analyse the problem of low activity of women and older people on EU labour market. Such approach determines the structure of the book.

The first part of the book is devoted to the description of the criteria that helped the authors select best practices and make characteristics of chosen practices. For each practice authors gave the short characteristics of the initiative, the target group and their measurable results.

The second part of the book deals with conditions of the best practices transfer. The authors described the essence of the best practices transfer and methodology for assessing the conditions of best practices implementation. However, the essential part of this chapter is questionnaire survey results, which was conducted among the project partners. The authors present legal, formal and financial terms of the best practices implementation related to the activation of senior citizens and women in four countries: Poland, Germany, Latvia and Lithuania. Moreover, readiness and commitment of public and private partners in the process of best practices implementing is discussed.

In the last part of book the transfers of best practices to four BSR countries are presented. For each best practices the authors described activities, which should to be undertaken to transfer the practices and analyzed benefits of the practices transfer. Additionally, minimal and optimal requirements for each best practices transfer were determined.

The authors hope that the results of research and analysis will allow the actual implementation of the proposed practices in selected countries in the Baltic Sea region. At the same time, the described methodology of identification of the transfer allows for flexible use for assessing the potential transfer of other practices in the promotion of women's economic activity and the elderly to the BSR countries.

Part I Determinants of best practices choice

1. Criteria for the best practices selection – the best practices, which increasing the participation of women on BSR labour market

The selection of good practice, supporting the participation of women on the EU labour market was not an easy choice. The authors decided to pursue three main criteria for making this selection.

Firstly, the best practices required to have features that the literature points to as fundamental of good practices such as effectiveness, efficiency, reflectiveness, innovation, versatility and ethics [Karwińska, Wiktor, 2008]. By effectiveness the actual contribution of good practice in the implementation of goals and objectives is meant. Efficiency is meant to achieve maximum results with determined inputs. Good practices are reflective, if it easy to conduct the process of their evaluation. The innovation of good practice manifests itself mainly in implementation of fresh, non earlier used ideas. In turn, the versatility of good practice includes the possibilities of the transfer and evaluation of this transfer.

Secondly, when choosing good practices supporting women's professional activity of EU labour market, the authors applied the principle of diversification. The authors wanted to show for which different entities in economy good practices can be applied. Good practice supporting the participation of women in the labor market can for example affect government's policy, hence the choice of good practice "Pay Equality Action Plan". Best practices can also be associated with the promotion of women's entrepreneurship, that is why we chose the practice "Fuuturis", or with the promotion of entrepreneurship among young women and youth, hence the choice of practice "Ambasadors for Women Enterprenership". The support of women's economic activity can be also pursued by supporting their education and it can increase their chances on the labor market. Therefore, we decided to choose practices "Femmale Future" and Women @ Work. At last, the achievement of higher labor market participation of women can be achieved through the promotion of self-employment among women and that is why we decided to choose the practice of "Women into Technology".

Thirdly, the authors want to choose such practices, which relate to the most important women's problems on the labor market in the countries to which best practices will be transferred. The first big problem is the low entrepreneurship among women. Self-employment[1] is considered in literature as the evidence of entrepreneurship or lack of opportunities to work as an employee. However, from the point of view of economy and the situation on BSR labor market this phenomenon is highly desired due to the evidence of the resilience of self-employment to the crisis, compared with paid employment [European Employment Observatory Review, 2010]. Generally, in the group of BSR countries[2] in year 2011 on average, about 13% men among all employed workers work as self-employed and only 7% of women prefer this form of work [Eurostat, 2011]. Therefore, we chose two practices: "Fuuturis" and "Ambassadors for Women Entrepreneurship".

The second problem is the unfavorable distribution of employment rates by sector, which provides a clear picture of the very different composition of female and male employment. Industry (specially ICT industry) is still the main work place for men, the services sector now provides the majority of female jobs. Men in all analyzed BSR countries are more likely than women to work in industry and agriculture and this situation hasn't changed much over the last decade. This is why we chose the best practice "Women in Technology".

The next problem on the BSR labour market is women's wages, which are usually lower than men. According to authors' analysis of wages in BSR nine countries, women earned gross and per hour less on average 17.2% in 2010 than men [Eurostat, 2012]. The unadjusted Gender Pay Gap[3] often varies between 15-22 % in most countries. Poland is the exception due to the lowest GPG (5,3 % in 2010), in turn, Estonia is known as a country with the highest GPG in Europe (27,6% in 2010). This is why we chose as very important to transfer the best practice "Pay Equality Action Plan".

The last large problem on BSR labor market is a big unemployment rate among young women i.e. in the age group of 15-24. Although, women are better educated than men in BSR region, the unemployment rates among women tend to be higher among the less educated women in the majority of countries, and tend to be lower

---

[1] A self-employed person is the sole or joint owner of the unincorporated enterprise (one that has not been incorporated i.e. formed into a legal corporation) in which he/she works, unless they are also in paid employment which is their main activity (in that case, they are considered to be employees). Self-employed people also include: unpaid family workers; outworkers (who work outside the usual workplace, such as at home); workers engaged in production done entirely for their own final use or own capital formation, either individually or collectively.

[2] Denmark, Germany, Estonia, Lithuania, Latvia, Poland, Finland, Sweden, Norway

[3] The unadjusted Gender Pay Gap (GPG) represents the difference between average gross hourly earnings of male paid employees and of female paid employees as a percentage of average gross hourly earnings of male paid employees

among the more educated workers. Thus, to increase the participation of especially young women in the labor market in the analyzed countries have chosen practice Female Future 'and Women @ Work to the transfer.

2. The women' best practices characteristics

Female future - mobilizing talents - a business perspective.

The NHO set up the Female Future project in 2003, and it lasted to 2008. The goals of the project were: to increase the percentage of women in decision-making process-es, in management and in boards in general; to cause that the private sector is viewed as an attractive place to work by women; to involve managers as prime movers in the process aimed at recruiting more women to executive positions and to board posts; to make executive responsibilities be more easily combined with family responsibili-ties - the balance between work and private life. The results were so good that the project owners decided to reintroduce the project. It is still running.

First step of the programme consisted in building a network of supportive ambassa-dors for the project. The NHO chose influential individuals to be ambassadors, peo-ple who could address the arguments why women in business are important. What's important, these ambassadors had to be both men and women.

The second step was the selection of companies (not women!), which are interested in the project. The enterprises were recruited into the programme, and the manager of the enterprise had to sign a contract. In these contracts the managers confirmed, that they would work to get one, two or more women into management, and into the board of directors. Also, the firms were obligated to nominate women- the candidates to Femmale Future programme from his/her own enterprises, to pay the costs relat-ing to participations in the Future Femmale programme, to facilitate for a good work-life balance.

Then the management of the companies, which decided to join the Female Future, would be asked to look for the female talents in their organization i.e. women that they meant have talent and potential to take on more challenging tasks and leader positions. The talents selected joined the Female Future programme for one year and become part of the strong Female Future network.

The Female Future training program consists of three parts: Personal leadership training, Board competence and rhetoric. The training lasted from 13 to 15 days. In addition, throughout the duration of the project, selected women worked together with the managers of companies.

The first phase of the Female Future Programme was carried out in four rounds from the autumn of 2003 until the spring of 2005. As of spring 2006, approximately 370 talents have gone through the Phase 1 programme. More than 200 women finished the extended programme in June of 2007. In the autumn year 20007, 250 more women participated in the extended programme, ending at the end of 2008. In summary, since the start up in 2004 more than 1151 hand-picked talented individuals have qualified to take on board posts and more demanding leadership tasks. Approximately 700 companies have joined the programme.

First results of the programme was very optimistic: 26 % of the participants in the national programme have been offered board positions during or after the Female Future Programmes. (larger PLCs companies, total 490 in Norway) and 50% have been offered board positions in several regional projects following their participation in the FF Project. This was an extremely good score and promising for all the smaller limited companies which are in majority in Norway. Last evaluation of the programme was done in May 2010: 62% of the participants were offered board positions or advanced in their management career. In 2014, 1350 women have participated in the programme. They have been reqruited from 750 companies. The results of the initial period have improved. 67 % of the participants received offers of board positions 9 months after completion of training.

The Female Future programme was appointed by ILO as one of the 10 best examples on Gender Equality. Japan, Austria and Uganda are initiating a Female Future program.

Women into Technology (WIT)

One of the largest problems related with the low participation of women in the labour market in the BSR countries is their under-representation in higher level ICT jobs. It is especially important, as the ICT sector is characterized by significant jobs growth dynamics.

Fife Women's Technology Centres (FWTC) were established in 1990 as a positive action initiative in order to train women who experienced real difficulty in obtaining work, so that they could rejoin the work force or take up further training opportunities. Their key priority was to widen horizons and raise aspirations by offering high quality training focusing on non-traditional areas, e.i. computing, electronics and IT.

The Programme "Women into Technology" started in year1992, which was aimed first of all at long term unemployed women, at lonely parents, black and minority ethnic women, and women with disabilities. The programme was financed in 26% from European Social Fund and the rest from local and national funding.

To be able to offer to the right path for entry into the labour market, the FWTC created the network of local partners. FWTC liaised with local specialist organizations (e.g. violence against women) to ensure all round support for women, with employers (e.g. local businesses, mostly SMEs, larger manufacturing companies, banks, authorities) and with other partners specializing in an exchange of job information, in the work placement or in identification of employment opportunity. FWTC chose Adam Smith College, which accredited all courses and provided the internal verification.

WIT Core Programme covers 2,5 days per week over 48 weeks and consists of modules in maths, communication, technology and IT. The integrated part of this programme is the course of personal development, which covers to confidence building, assertiveness and team work. After this part, women could choose their professional specialization and take part in "professional progress". For example the training" Office Administration" lasts 2 days per week over 24 weeks. It includes doing European Computer Driving Licence, improvement of practical office skills and the work placement (8-12 week) with a local employer. Another example of professional progression training is" the Technical IT programme". It consists of 2 days per week training over 48weeks in areas like Electric and Electronic Engineering, Computer Support, Network Support, Computing, Mechatronic Engineering). Additionally to the progression programmes, all women participate in personal development programme. It covers life coaching, personal presentation, CV writing, job search application and interview skills.

All courses are free of charge and additionally FWTC covers travel and childcare costs. If possible, the expenses related to the purchase of books or exams fees are covered by Fife Women's Technology Centres. However, the key success factors of training under WIT programme is the complex and integrated approach (materials, teaching methods), which guarantees a success path to the employment. Women, which took part in this project, indicated a supportive atmosphere connected with a high standard as a success factor. FWTC won the Best Practice Award in ICT and was commended for the Equal Opportunities Award at the European Social Fund Objective 3 Awards.

Fuuturi: Women entrepreneurs and managers in the future

This project was a continuation of three earlier projects of the same aim but previously focused on women start-ups. It started with a company Futuuri ('associated with the future') owned by a woman. This initiative ran between 2008-2011 and focused on developing existing businesses owned by women. Co-financed by the ESF, the North-Savo Centre for Economic Development, Transport and the Environment (ELY), the Regional Council of North Savo, Ylä-Savon Kehitys Oy, municipalities and companies.

The project was implemented by North Savo Education, the University of Kuopio and the Savonia University of Applied Sciences. The aims of the initiative were as follows:

— to promote women's entrepreneurship and management by speeding up the growth of enterprises and help the internationalization of the businesses, and also by supporting the participants' own business development projects,
— to develop the know-how and self-esteem of women entrepreneurs and managers has also been a goal. In addition, there has been a goal to develop each enterprise's knowledge-intensive service and product innovations,
— to support co-operation in networks among women.

Activities of the project included: a course with teaching methods like lectures, discussions, and study trips (excursions) built around seven separate modules (business management, implementation of a change in an enterprise, doing business electronically, internationalization, economic control of an enterprise, legal knowledge, marketing and communication). The same courses were held in 3 different locations for their benefit. The women also participated in volunteer-based development circles where they could exchange ideas, also had opportunity to gain support from other women working in the same sector of the economy. They could benefit from coaching. A fee of 500 Euros for three years was included. These activities were held during one meeting per week – sometimes in the evenings and sometimes at weekends.

The results of the initiative were as following:

— 196 women entrepreneurs have taken part in the initiative,
— more than 100 company owners got to plan,
— longer scale strategies and visions,
— more than 200 women entrepreneurs or leaders made a development plan and put these plans in action,
— at least 5 new product or service innovations were made in these companies,

— at least 10 new theses about women's entrepreneurship were prepared.

Pay Equity Action Plan

Each year, employers must prepare a plan describing their efforts to promote gender equality. The plan shall contain a survey of different measures which are required at the workplace and shall indicate which of such measures the employer intends to initiate or implement during the coming year":

— Working conditions: employers must take whatever steps may be required, insofar as their resources and general circumstances permit, to ensure that working conditions are suitable for both women and men.
— Employers shall facilitate the combination of gainful employment and parenthood with respect to both female and male employees.
— Employers shall take measures to forestall and prevent any employee from being subjected to gender-related harassment, to sexual harassment or to victimisation.
— Recruitment, etc.: employers shall, through training, skills development and other suitable measures, promote an equal distribution between women and men in various types of work and within different categories of employees.
— Employers shall endeavor to ensure that both women and men apply for vacant positions.
— Employers are required to formulate a pay equity action plan in order to ensure that remuneration is fixed on the basis of objective criteria that are common to all jobs. The employer must take into account following criteria: qualifications, responsibilities, efforts and working conditions."

Each year, employers are required to carry out a pay survey and analyze their pay policies and practices, even in cases where there was no disparity identified in the previous year. Following the survey, the employer must develop a pay equity action plan which includes the results of the pay survey, an analysis of the pay system and the planned approach to identify and correct pay inequalities in the system. The plan must list:the envisaged measures to eliminate the pay differentials, an estimate of the related costs and a timeframe that cannot exceed three years. A report concerning how the planned measures have been implemented must be included in the plan for the following year.

To measure the results of introduction of Pay Equality Action Plan, number of surveys have been carried out by JamO. An initial review covers 900 pay surveys carried out between 2001 and 2005. According to JamO, pay adjustments were made for at least 100 employers, or 11% of the total. Some 1000 employees had their pay adjusted on the basis of the principle of equal pay for equal work and 160 occupational groups, involving 9000 employees, had their pay adjusted in the context of equal pay for jobs of equal value. JamO, however, draws attention to the scant reliability of data regarding the number of employees affected. In 2004-2005, an additional survey was carried out in 50 organizations (10 from the municipal sector and 40 from the private sector) that had received support from JamO. The survey revealed that the pay adjustments that were required in 24 cases were all carried out (JamO 2005). This demonstrates that, even under a compulsory legal system, support and follow-up by specialized bodies is essential in ensuring fullest enforcement by companies. It is why JamO offers consultation and advisory service in relation to the development and implementation of pay equity action plans. With a view to helping SME to meet the requirements of the Act, JamO has also materials to guide SME's in the implementation of pay equity plans. Last survey done by JamO shows, that 25% of private companies had equality plans according to the law, and do 75% of public authorities.

Due to such great efficiency of Pay Equality Action Plan in Sweden, Finland adopted quite a similar system in year 2005.

Women@Work (W@W)

Initiative providing training and information for women. It gives women skill development via a learning programme, more ability to express their concerns about gender issues at workplace, in families and communities where they live, use their full potential in these environments This undertaking involves different bodies and industries. W@W has its own advisory group consisting of representatives from public, private and third sectors.

W@W involves employed women who have job experience and also focuses on more isolated women as a result of living in rural areas. It provides forum where ideas and opinions are exchanged. Also, it supports women to share experiences via networking thus making contacts and growing in confidence. It promotes women leadership via trainings and consultation on national and international level. The initiative allows to organize regular network meetings, speeches of guests, trainings and workshops.

The results of the project were amazing. The network has grown significantly in number of women members. Only within 6 months it grew from 420 in September 2009 to 816 in March 2010. 84% of women attending the initiative claimed that it boosted their confidence in terms of career progress, life progress, involvement in civic participation.

Ambassadors for Women's entrepreneurship

This initiative is a part of Swedish National Programme to Promote Women's Entre-preneurship .

Women Ambassadors are meant to work as role models to raise the interest about entrepreneurship, so that younger women t consider running a business as a career choice. The dominant image of a man as a picture of a small business owner-manager is aimed to be changed via this initiative

Ambassadors make attempts to disseminate the knowledge about entrepreneurship and also contribute to rise the interest of public media in women entrepreneurship issue.

Being ambassador carries: doing four voluntary jobs per year, such as speaking at different educational institutions such as schools or universities and doing study visits or hold personal meetings with women considering business start-up. Each ambas-sador is provided with a toolbox with all the useful materials to perform ambassador-ial visit. Ambassadors organize visits to their companies, do work shadowing, offer business training as well as mentoring.

Such ambassadors make an important mark in business and society as role models as they their stories and experiences. The ambassadors refer to different aspects of entrepreneurship, and so more women might consider themselves as entrepreneurs.

The ambassadors are varied in terms of the businesses they represent. They are locat-ed all over the country. Each Swedish county (official admin.region) has between 15-40 ambassadors. Cities like Stockholm, Göteborg and Malmö have more ambassadors than the rest of the counties. Other activities and measures in the whole programme include: providing information, business advice, business development, running ac-tions regarding business transfer, providing mentorship and supporting entrepreneur-ship among women academics

Results of the project are spectacular. Since 2008 more than 800 women entrepre-neurs have been selected as ambassadors however 1600 women entrepreneurs were interested to become ones. In the first three years around 82000 people were met by the ambassadors, of which 60 % were pupils at schools or university students. Euro-pean Network has been established and countries running initiative are altogether with Sweden: Albania, Belgium, Croatia, Cyprus, Denmark, France, Germany, Greece, Hungary, Iceland, Ireland, Italy, Luxembourg, Malta, Norway, Poland, Por-tugal, Romania, Serbia, Slovakia, Sweden and United Kingdom.

3. Criteria for the best practices selection – the best practices, which improve the elderly participation in the labour market

Aging is a real problem in the global scale. As it is said in the World Population Aging [2013] population ageing is taking place in nearly all the countries of the world. Ageing results from decreasing mortality and, most importantly, from the declines in fertility. This process leads to a relative reduction in the proportion of children, and to an increase in the share of people in the main working ages and of older persons in the population. The global share of older people (aged 60 years or over) increased from 9.2 per cent in 1990 to 11.7 per cent in 2013, and will continue to grow as a proportion of the world population, reaching 21.1 per cent by 2050.

Demographic change occurs differently in total population and working-age population: the latter shows much less ageing than the former but considerably more shrinking. Hence, whereas for individuals and societies the main issue until 2030 is population ageing, for firms it is shrinking of the labor force [Tivig et al. 2008].

The professional activation of persons aged 50 years and more becomes one of the most urgent challenges in all EU countries [*Ageing in the Twenty-First Century* 2012]. Due to the fact that the Europe 2020 Strategy [*A Strategy for smart, sustainable and inclusive growth* 2010] defines one of its aims as "75 % of the population aged 20–64 should be employed", the European countries take many initiatives to achieve this.

As the Eurostat data show, many of the Baltic Sea Region countries are too far from the proposed value of this indicator (see Table 1).

It should be noticed that the male employment rate is significantly higher than in the case of women.

Low level of education and qualifications as well as the lack of modern professional skills, especially ICT skills, are crucial reasons of not sufficient level of professional activity among elderly. To solve this problem, the Lifelong Learning Programme was started in 2006, as well as other educational initiatives run by different types of organizations.

Table 1. Employment rate[4] of older workers by gender in 2009-2010

	2005		2006		2007		2008		2009		2010	
	females	males	females	males	females	males	females	males	females	males	females	males
EU27	33,6	51,6	34,9	52,7	35,9	53,9	36,8	55	37,8	54,8	38,6	54,6
DK	53,5	65,6	54,3	67,1	52,4	64,9	50,1	64,6	50,9	64,1	52,5	62,7
EE	53,7	59,3	59,2	57,5	60,5	59,4	60,3	65,2	61,2	59,4	54,9	52,2
FI	52,7	52,8	54,3	54,8	55	55,1	55,8	57,1	56,3	54,6	56,9	55,6
DE	37,5	53,5	40,6	56,4	43,6	59,7	46	61,7	48,6	63,8	50,5	65
LV	45,3	55,2	48,7	59,5	52,4	64,6	56,7	63,1	53,3	53,1	48,7	47,6
LT	41,7	59,1	45,1	55,7	47,9	60,8	47,8	60,2	48,3	56	45,8	52,3
NO	60,1	70,8	61,6	73,1	64	73,8	64,2	74,1	64,6	72,8	65	72,2
PL	19,7	35,9	19	38,4	19,4	41,4	20,7	44,1	21,9	44,3	24,2	45,3
SE	66,7	72	66,9	72,3	67	72,9	66,7	73,4	66,7	73,2	66,7	74,2

Source: own calculation based on the Eurostat data [15.12.2012].

The analysis of statistics of participation in the continuous learning (the percentage of persons aged 24–64) show that in the Nordic countries it is much higher than in other countries of the Baltic Sea Region — it is also higher than the EU average (for 27 countries).

Quite similar situation is in the case of the employees' participation in supplementary training courses — in 2005 they were most popular in Denmark, Sweden and Finland. The most willing to participate in additional training were workers aged 25–54. By contrast, in Poland, Lithuania and Latvia, the proportion of employees participating in training courses was the lowest among all the countries of the Region — especially among people aged 55 and more.

Table 2. Percentage of population aged 25–64 participating in continuous education (continuing vocational training / CVT courses) — selected European countries

Region	2000	2001	2002	2003	2004	2005	2006	2007	2008	2009	2010	2011
EU27	7.1	7.1	7.2	8.5	9.2	9.6	9.5	9.3	9.4	9.3	9.1	8.9
DK	19.4	18.4	18.0	24.2	25.6	27.4	29.2	29.0	29.9	31.2	32.5	32.3
EE	6.5	5.4	5.4	6.7	6.4	5.9	6.5	7.0	9.8	10.5	10.9	12.0

---

[4] The employment rate of older workers is calculated by dividing the number of persons aged 55 to 64 in employment by the total population of the same age group. The indicator is based on the EU Labour Force Survey. The survey covers the entire population living in private households and excludes those in collective households such as boarding houses, halls of residence and hospitals. Employed population consists of those persons who during the reference week did any work for pay or profit for at least one hour, or were not working but had jobs from which they were temporarily absent.

FI	17.5	17.2	17.3	22.4	22.8	22.5	23.1	23.4	23.1	22.1	23.0	23.8
LV			7.3	7.8	8.4	7.9	6.9	7.1	6.8	5.3	5.0	5.0
LT	2.8	3.5	3.0	3.8	5.9	6.0	4.9	5.3	4.9	4.5	4.0	5.9
DE	5.2	5.2	5.8	6.0	7.4	7.7	7.5	7.8	7.9	7.8	7.7	7.8
NO	13.3	14.2	13.3	17.1	17.4	17.8	18.7	18.0	19.3	18.1	17.8	18.2
PL		4.3	4.2	4.4	5.0	4.9	4.7	5.1	4.7	4.7	5.3	4.5
SE	21.6	17.5	18.4			17.4	18.4	18.6	22.2	22.2	24.5	25.0

Source: Eurostat.

The main reasons of not participation in vocational courses and long-life learning are as follow [*Kształcenie dorosłych* 2009]:

— the cost of training,
— health reasons,
— family reasons.

Statistics show, that some of the barriers are closely related with the age (see Table 3).

Table 3. Types of obstacles by participation and age groups (2007) – respondents who did not participate but wanted to participate (in 27 EU countries)

	Total	From 25 to 34 years	From 35 to 54 years	From 55 to 64 years
Health or age	13.4	4.1	13.1	29.4
Lack of employer's support	16.3	15.6	18.1	11.6
Other	24.4	21.3	23.6	31.9
The respondent did not have time because of family responsibilities	36.6	37	38.9	28.6
The respondent did not have the prerequisites	13.3	12	13.7	14.2
The respondent was not confident with the idea of going back to something that resembles school	13.5	11	14.3	14.9
There was no training offered at reachable distance	18.6	20.5	18	17.4
Training conflicted with work schedule	35	34.9	38.3	24.1
Training was too expensive or the respondent could not afford it	28.3	34.4	27.4	21.3

Source: Eurostat.

All EU countries, including Baltic Sea Region, must undertake programmes and initiatives ensuring the increase of professional activity among persons 50+. As it was decided in 2002 in Madrid [*Political Declaration* 2002], in the process of professional activity promotion and prolongation, there should be involved different types of organizations from the regions and use different types of tools and methods. In the literature there are proposed some main directions on how to achieve the aim of older persons activity increase:

— all types of activities against the age discrimination (in the workplace and more widely – in the society) [Konopacka 2011],
— building up the awareness of aging process among politicians, entrepreneurs, managers and workers (including young persons) [Szukalski 2008],
— cooperation of all stakeholders of regional/national development (institutions responsible for educational, health care, entrepreneurs, labor unions, policy makers) on each stage of labor policy creation [Bielecka 2011],
— more flexibility of work conditions and work organization [Zeytinoglu 2005],
— promotion of entrepreneurship in older age [Kautonen 2008; Kautonen 2013].

The choice of good practices of elderly's professional activation (that were proposed to be transferred from Nordic countries to the others of Baltic Sea Region) should be read out as the result of deep experts' analysis. The statistics of aging and labor market situation were analyzed, as well as the literature and different EU legislative acts. Finally, there were five measures chosen to select the good practices:

— method of action,
— target group,
— intentional effects,
— level of intervention,
— type of action's organizer.

Authors defined two priorities in the process of choosing the good practices: they should show variety of possible actions and at the same time be quite easy to implement in counties fundamentally different that Nordic countries.

From the wide range of available solutions that were found in Nordic countries, authors chose for the transfer five good practices fulfilling the measures and complying the priorities (see Table 4).

Table 4. Measures and good practices chose to transfer

Measures	Characteristic	Good practices fulfilling the measures
Method of action	Development of entrepreneurship among persons aged 50+	Senior enterprises – experience never ages
	Flexibility of work organization (at the workplace)	Age management programme Flexible work practices
	Older persons' education	Higher Vocational Education
Target group	Employees aged 50+	Age management programme Flexible work practices Higher Vocational Education
	Unemployment and persons professionally inactive aged 50+ (including pensioners)	Senior enterprises – experience never ages
	Entrepreneurs/ employers	Age management programme Flexible work practices Senior policy in working life
	Social partners	Senior policy in working life
Intentional effects	Increasing the professional activity of persons aged 50+, including entrepreneur-ship promotion	Age management programme Flexible work practices Senior enterprises – experience never ages
	Building up the awareness of ageing process and its consequences	Senior policy in working life
Level of intervention	Enterprise	Age management programme Flexible work practices
	Region/country	Senior policy in working life
Type of action's organizer	Representatives of local/regional/national authorities	Senior policy in working life
	Social partners/ non-profit organizations	Senior policy in working life Senior enterprises – experience never ages Higher Vocational Education
	Education institutions	Higher Vocational Education
	Enterprises	Age management programme Flexible work practices

Source: own work.

4. The elderly best practices characteristics

Senior policy in working life

Senior policy in working life is based on a strategy of cooperation between relevant government agencies, major unions, employer associations and other professionals. The aims, and the most essential means, are presented in National Initiative for Senior Workers in Norway and The Tripartite Agreement on a More Inclusive Workplace – a contract signed up by the government and social partners.

CSP is responsible for coordinating the National Initiative. The Initiative was implemented in order to discourage older workers from retiring early and promote a longer working career. The target group are workers from the age of 45–50. The Initiative is part of the strategy aimed at top management of all the major unions, employers' associations and relevant government agencies. In brief, the Initiative consists of the following elements:

— Promote awareness of the potentials and resources older employees hold.
— Provide a better and more inclusive working environment for all workers.
— Create more cooperation among labour, employer and government organizations and authorities concerning senior policy.

The Tripartite Agreement on a More Inclusive Workplace is an initiative supported by the Government and its social partners to encourage people with different hindrances for employment, such as disability, early retirement pension or sickness benefits, to return to work, at least part time. The agreement, which lasted from October 2001 to 31 December 2005, had three objectives, which match the intention of the senior policy:

— Reduce sick leave by at least 20% by the end of the agreement period.
— Significantly increase employment among those that have minor disabilities.
— Increase the average age at which seniors choose to retire.

The aim is to achieve these objectives through voluntary agreements between company-level employers and the National Insurance Authority, with CSP as an important coordinator. To this end, the Centre has worked out a national plan in cooperation with the social partners to make individuals, companies and politicians aware of the advantages of hiring and retaining workers over the age of 45.

The majority of the senior policy initiatives are focused on promoting good personnel policy in general and create a more accommodating workplace. Senior policy is based upon experiences that show that personnel policy initiatives and other developing methods must have a life span perspective. Preventive efforts must therefore begin early in a person's career.

Senior enterprises – experience never ages

There are four main areas of the initiative:

— providing the knowledge and building the awareness - mainly training for people aged 50+ diagnosing and presenting the possibilities of their professional development, including starting the own business; distribution of information about tools available for new business owners – start-up's supporting system,
— substantive and organizational support for those persons 50+ who decide to start their own business including assistance in finding partners (training, financial assistance, a database of potential business partners),
— maintain the database of individuals aged 50 + interested in investing their funds in new business (Business Angels),
— cooperation with people 50 +: entrepreneurs, professionals in various fields of business, interested in providing advisory services (mentoring) for new entrepreneurs, including those aged 50 + (group and individual meetings with counselors).

Rising awareness' activities are addressed to three main target groups:

— those aged 50+ to present the possibilities given by the initiative;
— enterprise development agencies, financial institutions, agencies working with older people, younger entrepreneurs to show up the untapped potential that exists among older people;
— policy maker to convince them (politicians on different levels) to the idea of 50+ engagement in economy.

Starting and partnering activities deliver support instruments, that help older persons to start their new business (by themselves or in partnership with younger ones). The initiative supports older individuals to explore the personal, financial and commercial aspects involved in taking the first step into entrepreneurship. Those aged 50+ may consider starting a business in partnership with a younger individual. The drive and enthusiasm of the younger person would then benefit from the wider knowledge, experience, networks and resources of the older individual.

Investing and acquiring, those are activities focused on "using" the finances of successful 50+, who represent an excellent potential source of investment. In many respects the most rewarding form of investment is when an individual aged 50+ invests in a business sector that he/she knows well and brings expertise, as well as money, to the new business (star-up).

Advising area is very important part of the initiative. Suitably qualified and experienced older people provide the support to owner managers of new and existing businesses. They share with their knowledge and experience with the youngers and help them in designing strategic plans for their companies development.

The initiative is supported by EU funds (INTERREG IVB NWE). It's run by The Senior Enterprise Association, which has variety of membership categories including individuals and organizations from the public, private and NGO sectors and a very wide membership scope is encouraged. The lead partner is The Mid East Regional Authority, but initiative is also support by royal family. One of the partners is PRIME – The Prince's Initiative for Mature Enterprise.

Flexible work practices

Kronoberg County Council's most important responsibility relates to health care, and around 85% of its activity is devoted to medical and health services. The council represents the largest employer in the county of Kronoberg, with 5,280 employees, 80% of whom are women. The five largest staff categories are nurses (28%), assistant nurses (15%), doctors (9%), keepers (9%) and administrators (8%). Employees' average age is 47 years. Almost 20% of the workforce are aged between 50 and 59 years, almost 28% are over 55 years and more than 11% are aged over 60 years. The council expects many employees to retire within 10 years. Staff turnover is currently 6.7%.

The main problem in personnel policy recognized by the council is that 40% of health care employees will leave the labour market within 15 years. Therefore, the council depends on its older employees for both skills and staffing.

Presented initiative includes:

— skills training for managers – a plan for manager training is being prepared to ensure that the original initiative is implemented in everyday activities,

— using pensioners as substitutes–employees at two of the council's facilities can continue to work as substitutes after retirement when they reach 64 years of age,
— career planning at 55 years of age,
— mentorship – one of the council's facilities has a structured skills-transfer programme,
— enhancing workers' employability – the county council aims to keep all workers' skills up-to-date to preserve their employability,
— learning centre – the council has set up local learning centres that use modern techniques and where workers can pursue formal education or other training, flexibly and at their own pace,
— validation – the council plans to validate experience-based knowledge so that workers can more easily move between job categories or employers,
— career and advice centre – the council plans to set up a career and advice centre to facilitate career planning.

Higher Vocational Education

Higher vocational programme may be of 200 vocational credits (equivalent to one full academic year) or 400 vocational credits, corresponding to two full academic years.

The Swedish National Agency is responsible for allocation of funds to this type of education in Sweden.

Currently, there are 1100 courses like this in Sweden, realized by different types of educational organizations (Sensus runs only one course – International Key Account Manager).

Procedure of preparing the Higher Vocational Education Programme:

— steering group (different regional stakeholders, e.g. entrepreneurs, representatives of local authorities, representatives of trade unions etc.) execute an analysis of the regional labour market's situation, especially in the field of scarce occupations;
— teachers, coaches, mentors and trainers in the course – high level specialists, practitioners from different types of institutions;
— programme aim – formation of mainly practical high professional skills;
— educational organization interested in running such a course must apply for funds to Swedish National Agency – one application for two editions of the course;
— course group – 30–35 persons;

— courses last 2–4 semesters (10 hours of classes per week + own projects work + learning in work environment)

Higher Vocational Education Programme's result: more very highly qualified specialists, needed in regional labour market and ready to take over the managerial responsibilities.

Part II Conditions of the best practices transfer

1. Introduction

One of the tasks of the Project Partners was identifying best practices in strengthening the economic activity of women and older people in the context of developing the competitiveness and innovation of SMEs, as well as determining the possibilities and conditions of their transfer. Transfer in this case is understood as the implementation of selected and described solutions in enterprises and public organizations from all the Baltic Sea Region (BSR) countries.

The co-ordination of the task and achieving the expected results of the project in this part was the responsibility of the Gdańsk University of Technology (PP10). Due to the complexity of the data analysis process (the data is often available only in the vernaculars) and the need to define specific conditions for the implementation of individual solutions in different countries, all project partners participated in performing the task[5].

This report focuses on presenting the diagnosis methodology related to the possibilities and the conditions of selected good practices implementation in BSR countries adopted in the course of the research, as well as on discussing the obtained results.

2. Research methodology

2.1. The essence of the transfer of best practices

Best practices are solutions that due to the use of specific materials, technologies, procedures etc., allow for obtaining better results than in the case of other materials, technologies, procedures, etc. Best practices are behaviour standards and reference points for other entities interested in the implementation of similar activities. Enterprises and public organizations most often use best practices to attain satisfactory market position and ensure competitiveness cheaper and faster, as compared to the circumstances in which they would have to create specific solutions on their own. Searching for best practice which could be a model is usually a task of the concerned entity (enterprise or public organization) and results from a thorough self-assessment

---

[5] The exceptions were the Minsk and Brest Departments of the Belarusian Chamber of Commerce and Industry, which remained inactive in the project during the performance of the task due to formal reasons.

and benchmarking process [Bogan, English 1994]. More and more often, however, the best practices are subject to accreditation and the information about them is publicly available [Nash, Ehrenfeld 1997].

Transfer of best practices is one of the most difficult processes in the management of organizations. The solutions which proved effective in organization Y cannot be simply copied and implemented in organization X. It must be taken into account that the effect achieved by organization Y is affected by a number of its idiosyncratic circumstances, both dependent and independent of Y. Due to other circumstances and the internal structure of organization X, applying the same solutions and actions as in the case of organization Y may yield quite different results. Caution in the use of best practices results from the situational approach in management. Representatives of this perspective focus on the description and analysis of a variety of both internal and external conditions, the nature and interconnectedness of which justify the application of a given organizational model [Kacznmarek, Sikorski 1998, p.24]. The basic premise of the situational approach is the relativism of the organizational rules and principles, i.e. assuming that they apply only in relation to certain categories of situations [Stanryła, Trzciniecki 1986].

As reported by the American Productivity and Quality Centre, the main limitations for effective implementation of best practices in follower organizations are [http://www.themanagementor.com/kuniverse/kmailers_universe/manu_kmailers/bp_ensurecomp3.htm]:

— insufficient involvement of the management in the process of identifying best practices and their implementation,
— incorrect choice of the model solution, being unsuitable for a given problem,
— silo thinking and lack of mutual communication between the different departments of the organization,
— too short a time for learning the given best practice and the conditions for its success, as well as the fast pace of implementation and too high expectations regarding the quick development of positive effects,
— missing or insufficient experience of employees preventing or slowing down the effective implementation of a best practice.

Among the critical success factors of best practice transfer in enterprises, the professionals distinguish i.a. selecting an appropriate model solution, understanding the determinants of its effective implementation or ensuring favourable conditions for the implementation in the follower organization (see Table 1).

Table 1. Critical conditions of best practice implementation success

Related to the best practice chosen for implementation	common goal of best practice and the implementing enterprise
	appropriate choice, aligned with the implementing enterprise competences
Related to the workforce of the implementing enterprise	suitable qualifications of the workforce enabling the implementation
	proper selection of the team responsible for the implementation
Related to the management of the implementing enterprise	internal communication and promotion of best practice ideas
	creating an environment conducive to the best practice being implemented and willing to share its expertise
	providing the infrastructure necessary for the implementation
	management commitment

Source: [Jarrar, Zairi 2000].

2.2. Selection of best practices

One of the areas of activity within the project was the selection of best practices related to strengthening the economic activity of women and seniors in the context of developing the competitiveness and innovation of SMEs. Due to the Scandinavian enterprises' considerable experience in this area, the best practices were sought among them with view to possible future implementation in the remaining BSR countries, mainly in Lithuania, Latvia, Germany and Poland.

A comprehensive analysis of the solutions used mainly by Scandinavian companies and public organizations to combine the economic activity of women and seniors with enterprise innovation, as well as complex consultations with other partners of the project, allowed GUT to select 11 best practices: 6 related to women's activity and 5 based on solutions used in the case of older workers (see Table 2).

Table 2. Best practices selected for implementation

Focused on using the potential of women	Female future
	Women into Technology
	Pay Equity Action Plan

	Fuuturi: Women entrepreneurs and management future
	Women@Work
	Ambassadors for Women's entrepreneurship
Focused on using the potential of seniors	Senior policy in working life
	Senior enterprises – experience never ages
	Age management programme
	Flexible work practices
	Higher Vocational Education

Source: own work.

A synthetic description of all the best practices selected as model solutions for implementation in remaining BSR countries is presented in the Annex to this report.

3. Methodology for assessing the conditions of best practices implementation

In order to diagnose the possibilities and conditions of selected best practices implementation in enterprises from chosen BSR countries, a questionnaire survey was conducted. The questionnaire consisted of 20 close-ended questions with such answers as: "definitely disagree", "rather disagree", "I have no opinion", "rather agree", "definitely agree" and three open-ended questions. Respondents answering the questions in the questionnaire referred to each of the best practices separately.

The close-ended questions covered four main areas of conditions influencing the implementation in selected countries:

— financial issues, including the availability of aid from the European Union for the implementation of similar solutions,
— formal and legal issues,
— alignment of the best practice issues (economic activity of women and seniors in the context of developing innovation and competitiveness of SMEs) with the objectives and activities of the central, regional and local authorities and enterprises,
— readiness and commitment of public and private partners in the implementation process of the outlined best practices.
— In the open-ended questions, the respondents could, on the other hand:
— comment on other similar projects / practices implemented in their countries of origin,

— identify actions which would contribute to the growth of interest in the implementation of the proposed best practices,
— propose some forms of support that would be necessary in case a decision to implement the proposed best practices is made.

12 project partners from Finland, Sweden, Norway, Poland, Lithuania, Latvia, Belarus and Germany were invited to take part in the research. Responses were received from 9 of them: Germany (3), Poland (2), Finland (1), Norway (1), Sweden (1), Latvia (1) and Lithuania (1). No response was obtained from the Partner from Belarus.

The replies of partners from Poland, Lithuania, Latvia and Germany were particularly valuable because it is in these countries where some best practices would be implemented. The replies of partners from the Nordic countries were treated as supplementary information serving to specify the nature and terms of best practice implementation more accurately..

4. Results of the research

4.1. The financial terms of the implementation of best practices for the seniors

One of the problems hindering the implementation of best practices related to the activity of seniors is related to financial issues (see Figures 1 and 2), including the availability of an external (public or private) funding for this type of activity (see Figures 3 and 4), as well as the limited access to information on potential sources of funding (see Figure 5).

Figure 1. In our country/region there are no or very little own sources among institutions potentially interested in implementing this kind of solution – number of answers in total

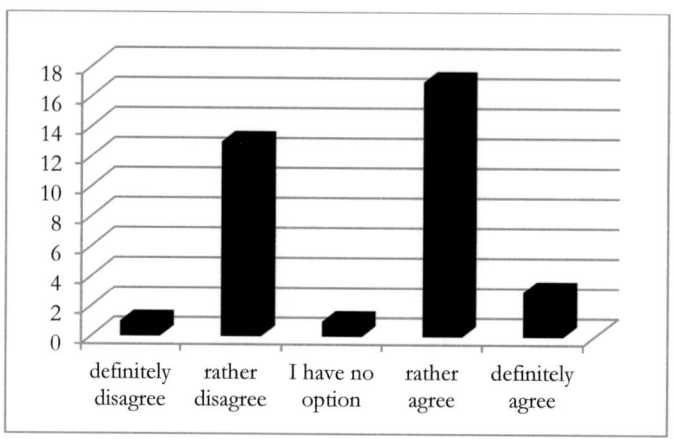

Source: own work.

Figure 2. In our country/region there are no or very little own sources among institutions potentially interested in implementing this kind of solution – number of answers in relation to each best practice*

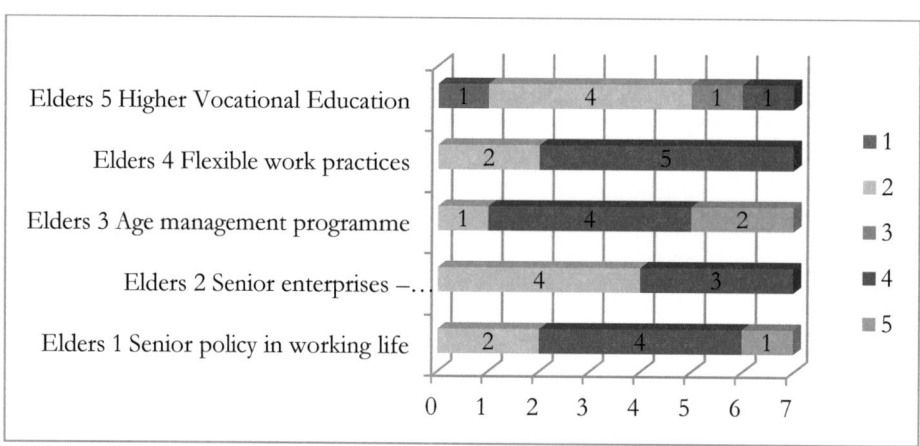

* 1- definitely disagree, 2- rather disagree, 3- I have no option, 4- rather agree, 5- *definitely agree*
Source: own work.

In 20 cases, the answer to the question related to the problems with obtaining financial resources for the implementation of activities similar to those described as best practices was *agree* or *rather agree*. 14 responses stated that there should be no problem with obtaining funds for implementation. Indicating financial issues was significantly dependent on the type of best practice.

Figure 3. In our country/region there is a limited access to external (public/private) sources for financing this kind of projects – number of answers in total

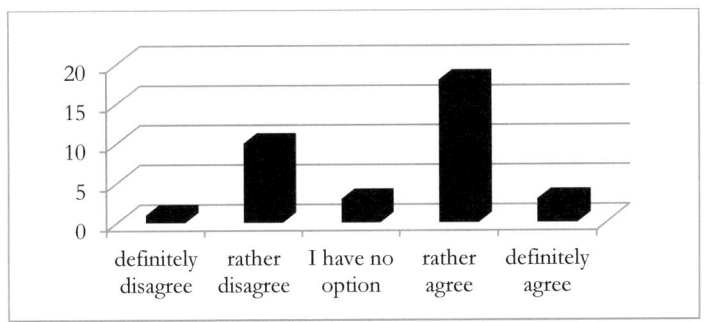

Source: own work.

Figure 4. In our country/region there is a limited access to external (public/private) sources for financing this kind of projects – number of answers in relation to each best practice*

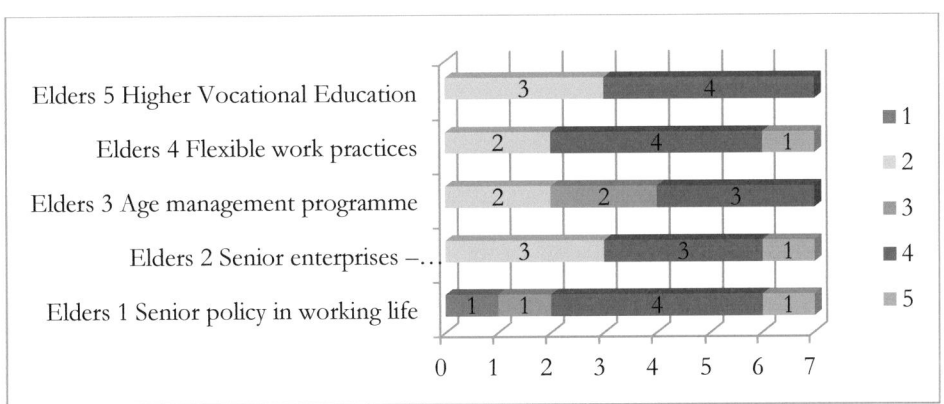

* 1- definitely disagree, 2- rather disagree, 3- I have no option, 4- rather agree, 5- definitely agree
Source: own work.

The financial barrier associated with limited access to external funding was identified in 21 cases. As in the case of the limited own resources, a dependence on the type of best practice can be seen.

Figure 5. In our country/region there is a limited access to information about potential external financial sources for this kind of projects – number of answers in total

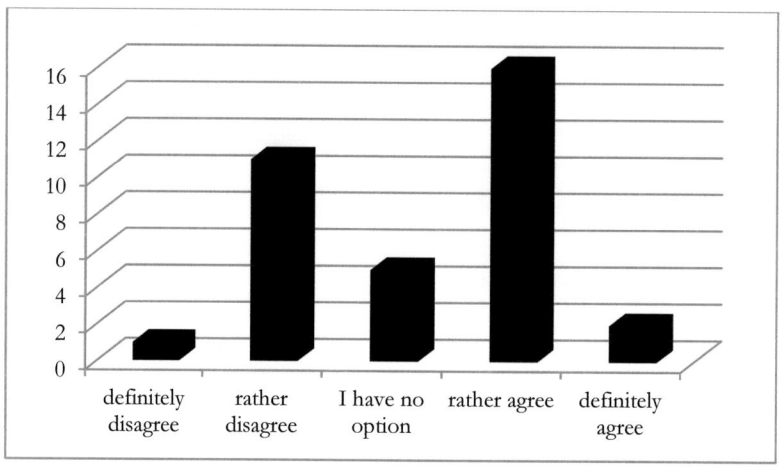

Source: own work.

As the research showed, access to information about external sources of funding can still be a problem. If case of this response, a significant variation due to the respondents' countries of origin is visible. On the other hand, the type of best practice did not affect the responses in any way in this case.

4.2. Similarity of best practices related to the seniors with the objectives and activities of the central government, regional and local authorities and enterprises

The research results show that both the need to boost enterprise innovation and competitiveness (see Figure 6) and the need to activate the seniors (see Figure 7) are perceived by the respondents' countries of origin societies as major economic and social problems.

Figure 6. In our country/region innovation level is not regarded as a problem – number of answers in total

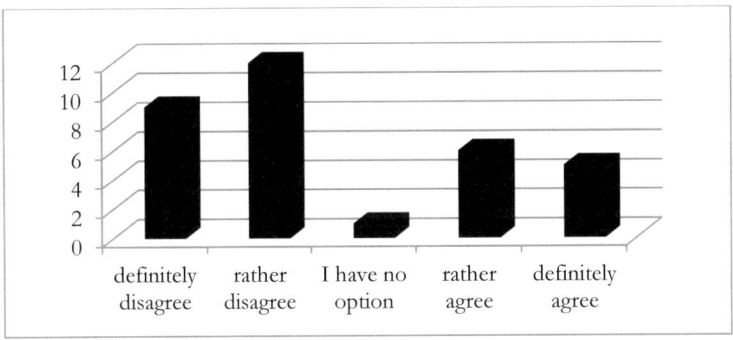

The suggested best practices have been chosen so that they not only strengthen the economic activity of seniors but also encourage the growth of innovation in the country / region. 11 responses obtained in the study indicated that the level of enterprise innovation is not perceived as a problem (they came mostly from German partners, which can be explained by the fact that German companies are recognized as innovation leaders). In 21 responses, however, innovation was recognized as a problem.

Figure 7. In our country/region low professional activity of the elderly is not regarded as a problem – number of answers in total

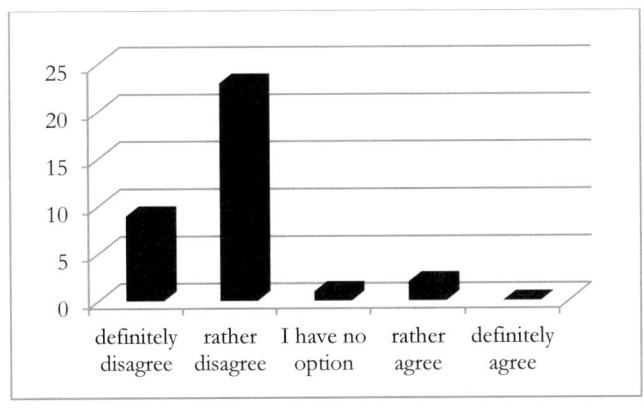

Most responses confirm that in the BSR countries the problem of low economic activity of seniors is noticed and seen as requiring urgent action.

The study allowed also for concluding that the issue of enterprise innovation and economic activation of seniors lies in the very centre of regional and national policies. Both the national and the regional authorities show an interest in the issues of senior activity (Fig. 9) and the ideas presented in the best practices are not in conflict with regional and national strategies (see Figure 8).

Figure 8. The aim and guidelines of the proposed practice are contradictory with national/local policies (and so are strategic documents) – number of answers in total

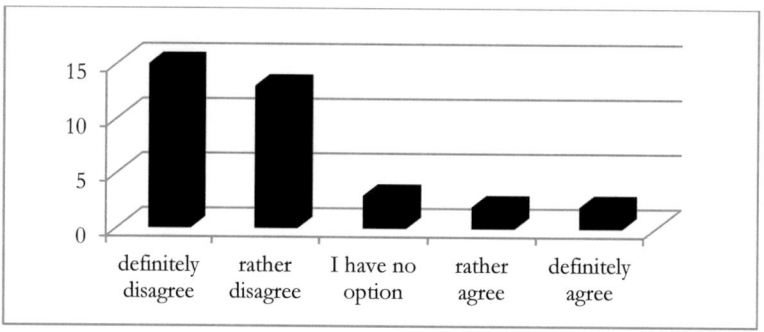

Source: own work.

Figure 9. In our country/region there is no interest among local government/institutions/partners in implementing this kind of practice – number of answers in total

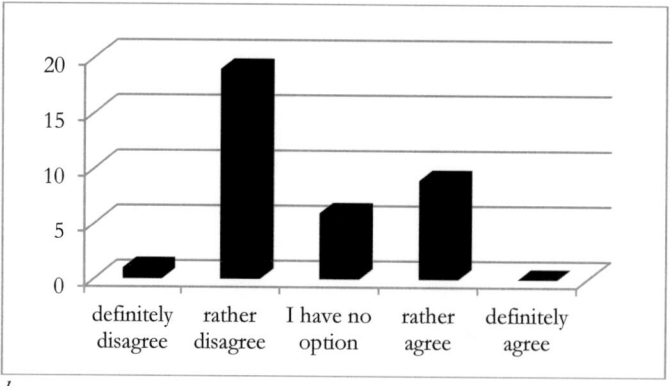

Source: own work.

4.3. Formal and legal conditions for implementation of best practices related to the activation of senior citizens

The study shows that the implementation of the best practices proposed in project should not be limited by formal and legal conditions being in place in individual countries, with the exception of flexible forms of employment of seniors and building a comprehensive system of gradual withdrawal from work (senior policy in working life). In both cases, the solutions have been developed in the Nordic countries several decades ago and thoroughly tested since then. Among other countries, also in Poland there is currently a discussion on this kind of solutions. However, the strong position of trade unions does not allow for their expedited implementation, because they are considered by many to be disadvantageous for employees.

Figure 10. In our country/region there are no regulations that allow for implementation of this project – number of answers in total

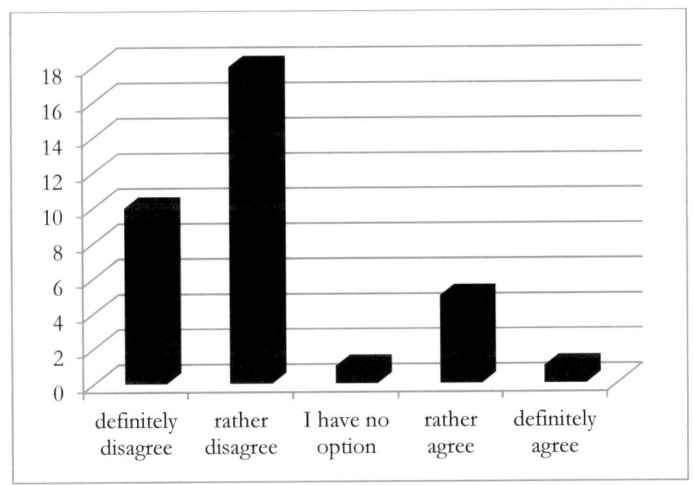

Source: own work.

Figure 11. In our country/region there are no regulations that allow for implementation of this project – number of answers in relation to each best practice*

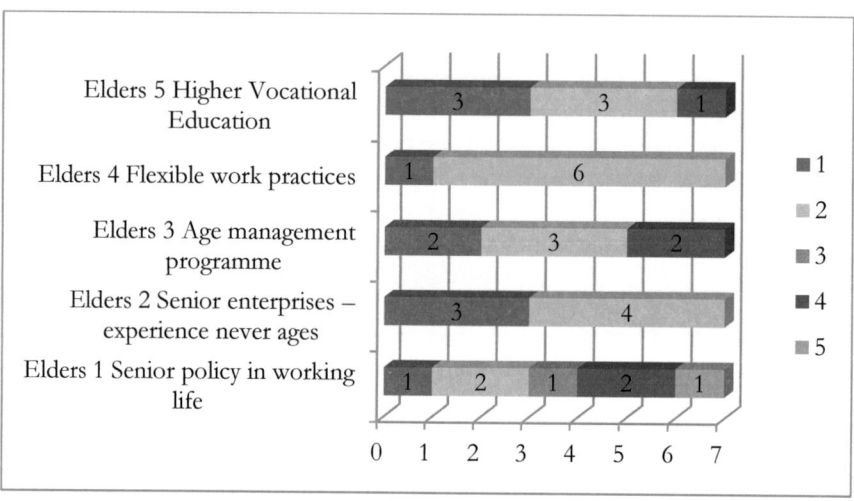

* 1- definitely disagree, 2- rather disagree, 3- I have no option, 4- rather agree, 5- definitely agree
Source: own work.

Figure 12. In our country/region the regulations are not flexible enough and so do not allow to take into account particular actions and solutions that are a crucial element of this practice – number of answers in total

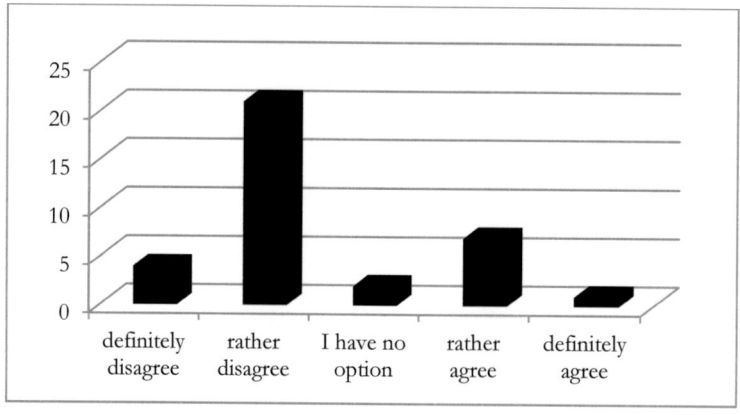

Source: own work

Figure 13. In our country/region the regulations are not flexible enough and so do not allow to take into account particular actions and solutions that are a crucial element of this practice – number of answers in relation to each best practice*

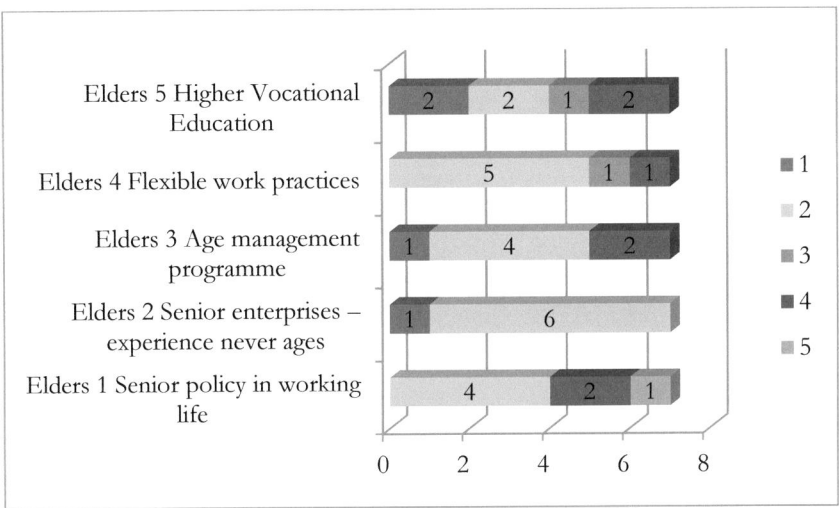

* 1- definitely disagree, 2- rather disagree, 3- I have no option, 4- rather agree, 5- definitely agree
Source: own work.

In case of most of the best practices the respondents did not observe any toughening of regulations that prevent their implementation. In case of the practice of implementing the comprehensive senior citizen policy, the respondents drew attention to the low flexibility of the legal system.

According to participants, the implementation of the proposed best practices could sometimes result in the need to obtain additional permits/licenses for the interested institutions (12 replies suggesting that this may be the case). Just as in the previous question, in their opinion mainly the introduction of a comprehensive senior citizen policy would require such solutions (see Figure 14).

Figure 14. Undertaking this practice requires additional permissions by institutions implementing it – number of answers in relation to each best practice*

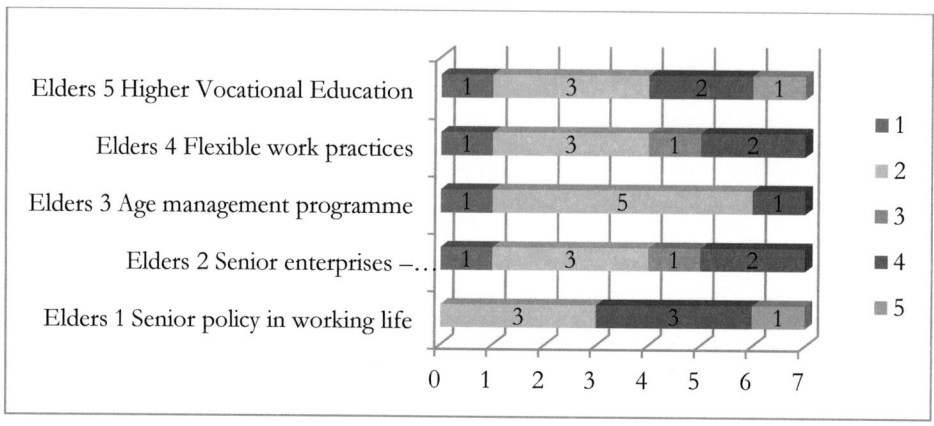

* 1- definitely disagree, 2- rather disagree, 3- I have no option, 4- rather agree, 5- definitely agree
Source: own work.

4.4. Readiness and commitment of public and private partners in the process of implementing best practices related to the activation of senior citizens

According to the respondents, the proposed best practices are not opposed to the traditional way of thinking and acting related to solving problems of economic inclusion of people who are disadvantaged in the labour market (see Figure 15 and 16).

Figure 15. This practice is contradictory to traditional way of thinking and acting in our country/region in terms of integration of economically excluded groups into the labour market – number of answers in total

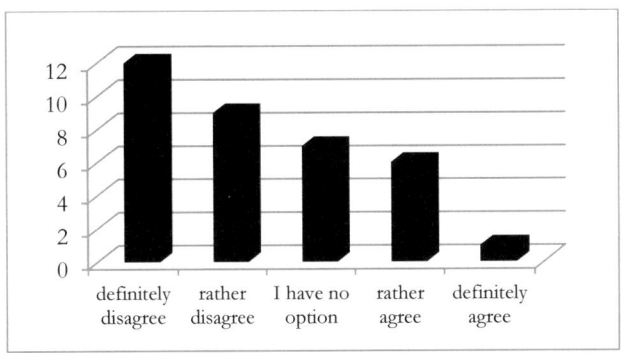

Source: own work.

Figure 16. This practice is contradictory to traditional way of thinking and acting in our country/region in terms of integration of economically excluded groups into the labour market – number of answers in relation to each best practice*

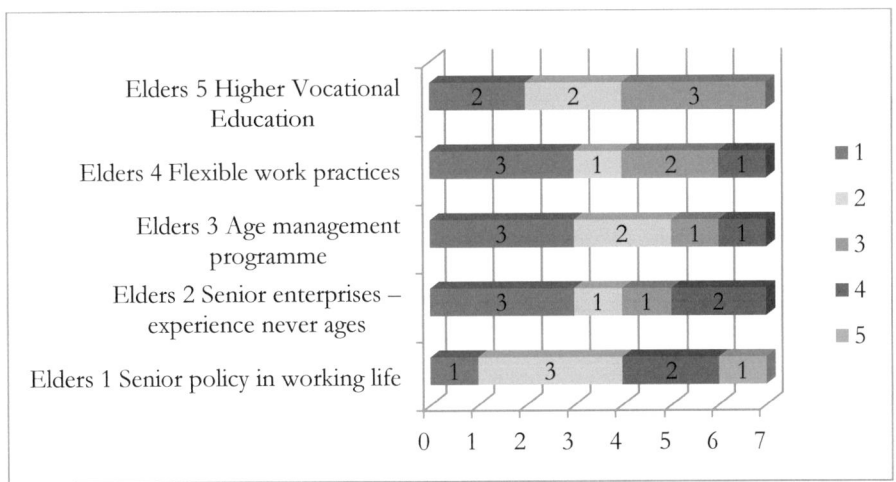

* 1- definitely disagree, 2- rather disagree, 3- I have no option, 4- rather agree, 5- definitely agree
Source: own work.

The main problem in the process of implementation of the proposed best practices related to the activity of senior citizens may be the missing or insufficient motivation of potential partners responsible for their implementation (see Figure 19), as well as insufficient qualifications (see Figure 17). Lack of adequate competence / qualifications / experience among the partners was identified as a barrier 10 times, so attention should be paid to this issue in determining the precise conditions of implementation in specific countries.

Figure 17. In our country/region local government/institutions/partners do not have sufficient experience, skills and competences necessary for implementing this kind of practice – number of answers in total

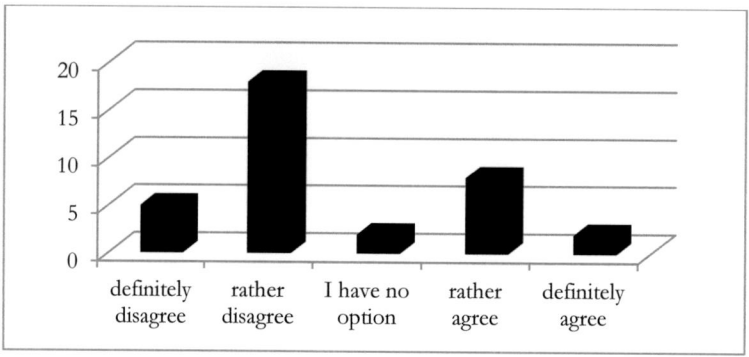

Source: own work.

Figure 18. In our country/region local government/institutions/partners do not have sufficient experience, skills and competences necessary for implementing this kind of practice – number of answers in relation to each best practice*

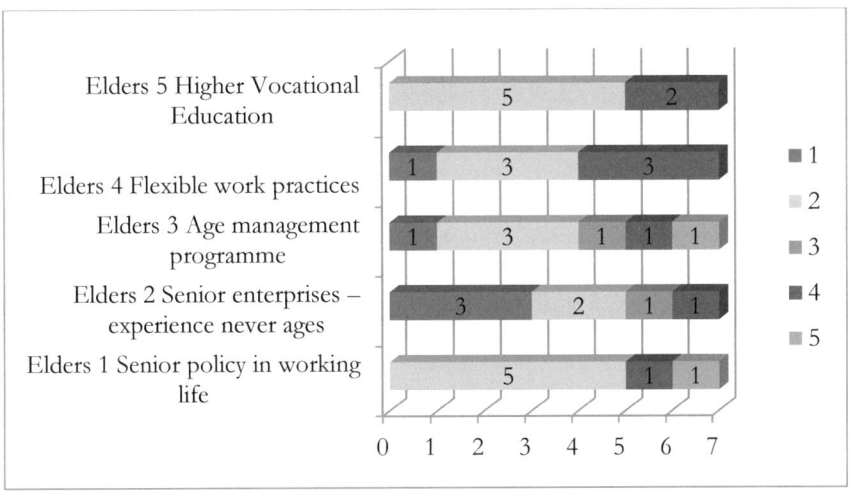

* 1- definitely disagree, 2- rather disagree, 3- I have no option, 4- rather agree, 5- definitely agree
Source: own work.

Figure 19. In our country/region potential beneficiaries of such practice would not display sufficient motivation to participate in this practice/there are not enough incentives for participating in this practice – number of answers in total

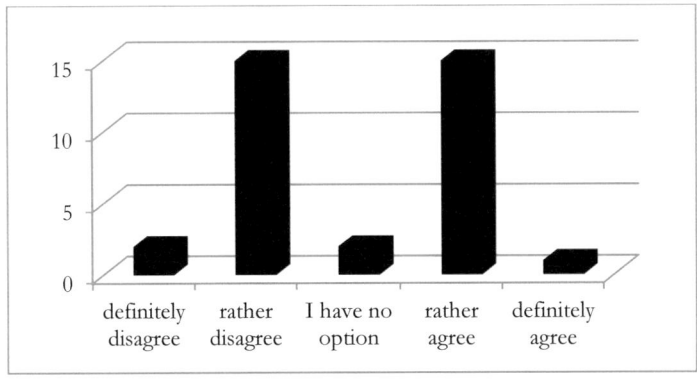

Source: own work.

Figure 20. In our country/region potential beneficiaries of such practice would not display sufficient motivation to participate in this practice/there are not enough incentives for participating in this practice – number of answers in relation to each best practice*

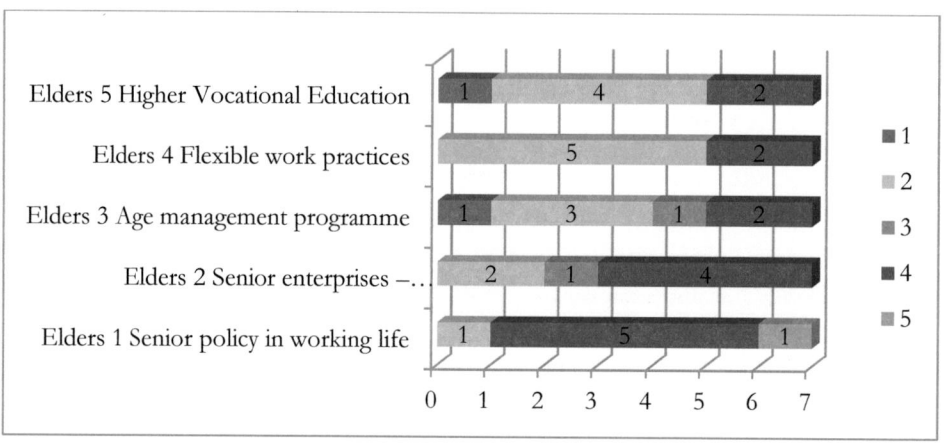

Source: own work.

Lack of motivation to participate in the project is by far the most often cited obstacle for practices 1 and 2.

Another reason for compromising the implementation of best practices is the fact that similar initiatives have already been implemented in the given country. The study shows, however, that in 22 cases there was no such restriction.

Figure 21. In our country/region there are already similar practices like this one and there is no need to implement this one – number of answers in relation to each best practice*

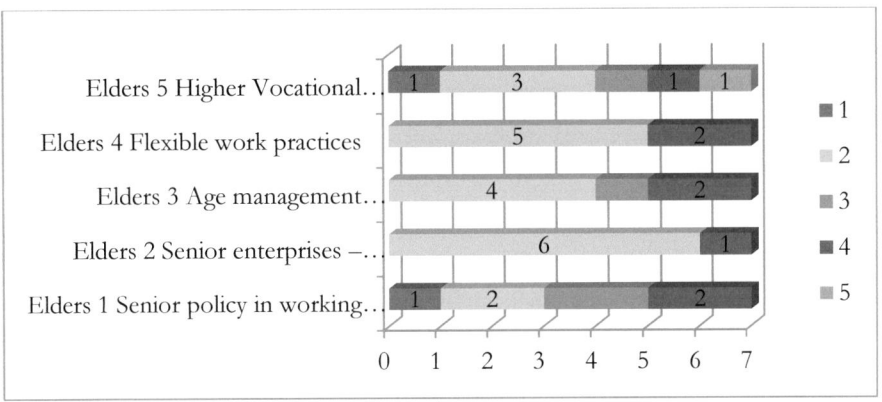

* 1- definitely disagree, 2- rather disagree, 3- I have no option, 4- rather agree, 5- definitely agree
Source: own work.

4.5. Financial issues and the process of implementation of best practices related to activation of women

As in the case of best practices aimed at activation of senior citizens, also for the best practices presenting solutions that activate women one of the main barriers for implementation is finance (see Figure 22), including limited access to external (public or private) sources of funding such projects (see Figure 24).

Figure 22. In our country/region there are no or very little own sources among institutions potentially interested in implementing this kind of solution – number of answers in total

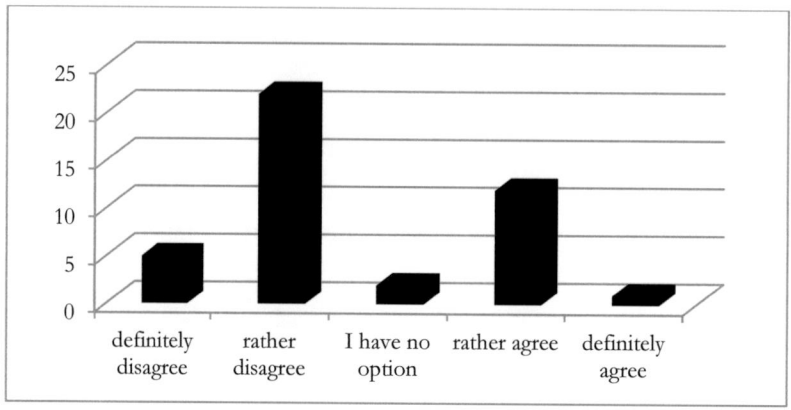

Source: own work.

Figure 23. In our country/region there are no or very little own sources among institutions potentially interested in implementing this kind of solution – number of answers in relation to each best practice*

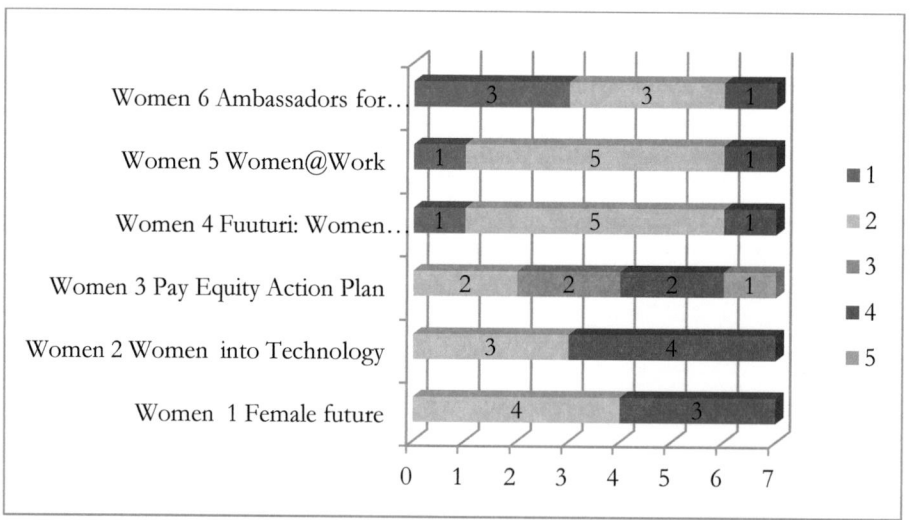

* 1- definitely disagree, 2- rather disagree, 3- I have no option, 4- rather agree, 5- definitely agree
Source: own work.

Figure 24. In our country/region there is a limited access to external (public/private) sources for financing this kind of project – number of answers in total

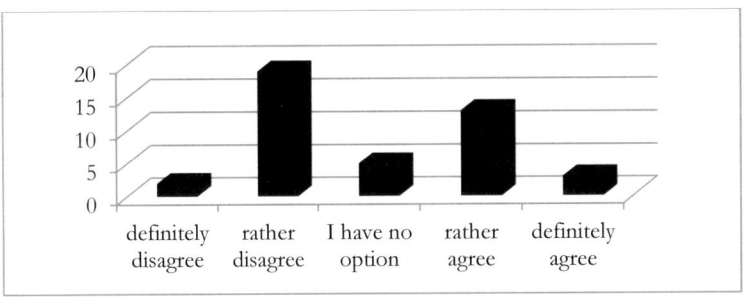

Source: own work.

The financial barrier associated with limited access to external funding was identified in 15 cases. As in the case of the question related to the availability of own resources, a dependence on the type of best practice can be seen.

Also quite interesting seem the responses to the question regarding the availability of information about the possibilities of acquiring financial resources for projects similar to the standard ones. First of all, access to information about external funding sources is, in respondents' opinion, varied in case of each of the practices. Secondly, this barrier is indicated relatively less frequently than in the case of the best practices concerning seniors (cf. Fig. 25 and 26).

Figure 25. In our country/region there is a limited access to information about potential external financial sources for this kind of project – number of answers in total

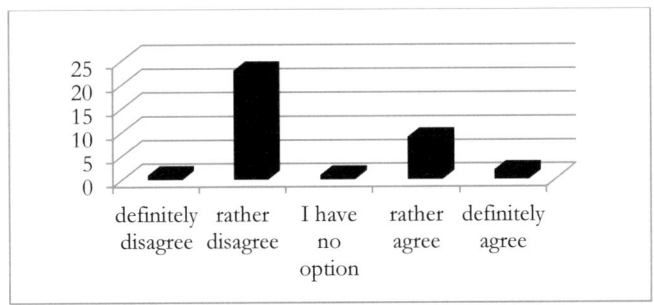

Source: own work.

Figure 26. In our country/region there is a limited access to information about potential external financial sources for this kind of project – number of answers in relation to each best practice*

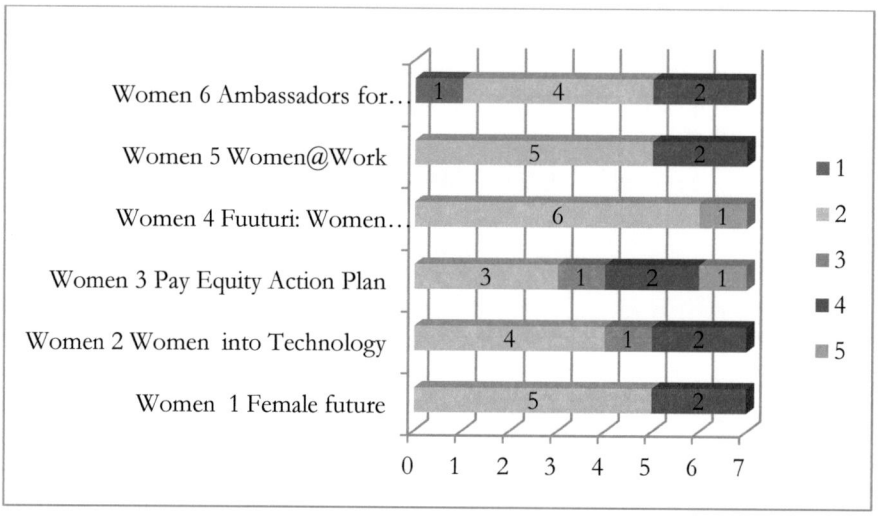

* 1- definitely disagree, 2- rather disagree, 3- I have no option, 4- rather agree, 5- definitely agree
Source: own work.

4.6. Similarity of best practices related to women with the objectives and activities of the central government, regional and local authorities and enterprises

The issue of women's low economic activity in the project partners' countries of origin is seen unambiguously as an important socio-economic issue which requires specific intervention.

Figure 27. In our country/region low economic activity of women is not regarded as a problem – number of answers in total

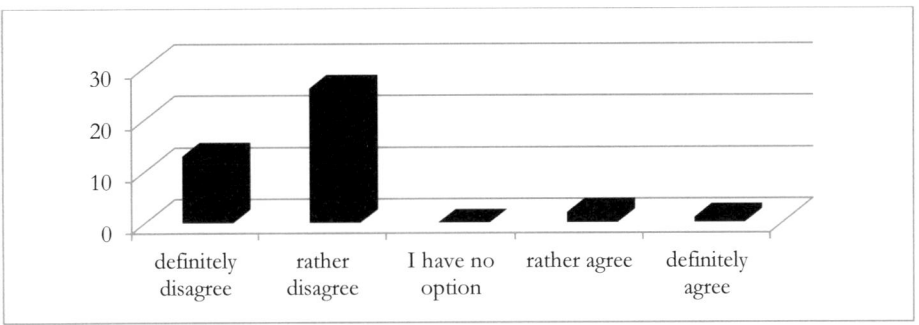

Source: own work.

The activities which activate women economically, in addition to enhancing innovation and competitiveness of the economy as a whole, are consistent with the goals of national and regional strategic documents (see Figure 28). At the same time, some respondents pointed that the local authorities and the social partners from the region do not show sufficient interest in implementing such initiatives (see Figure 29). Anyway, the implementation of practices 4, 5 and 6 should cause fewest problems. This barrier was indicated 13 times (see Figure 30).

Figure 28. The aim and guidelines of the proposed practice are contradictory with national/local policies (and so are strategic documents) – number of answers in total

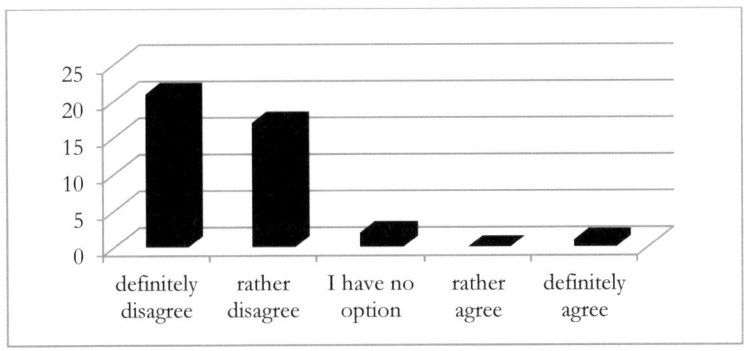

Source: own work.

Figure 29. In our country/region there is no interest among local government/institutions/partners in implementing this kind of practice – number of answers in total

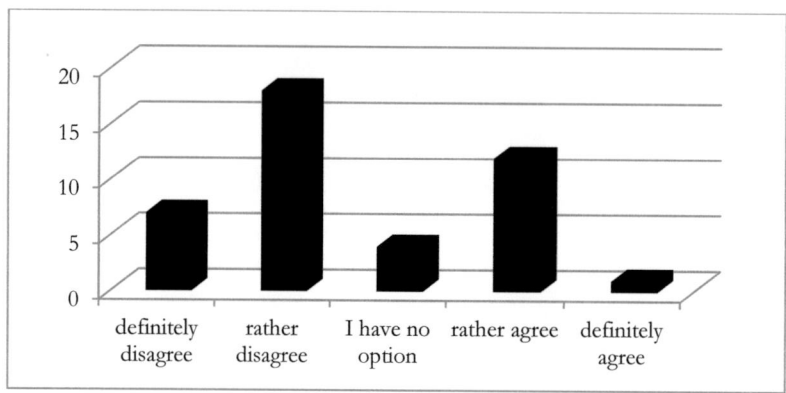

Source: own work.

Figure 30. In our country/region there is no interest among local government/institutions/partners in implementing this kind of practice – number of answers in relation to each best practice*

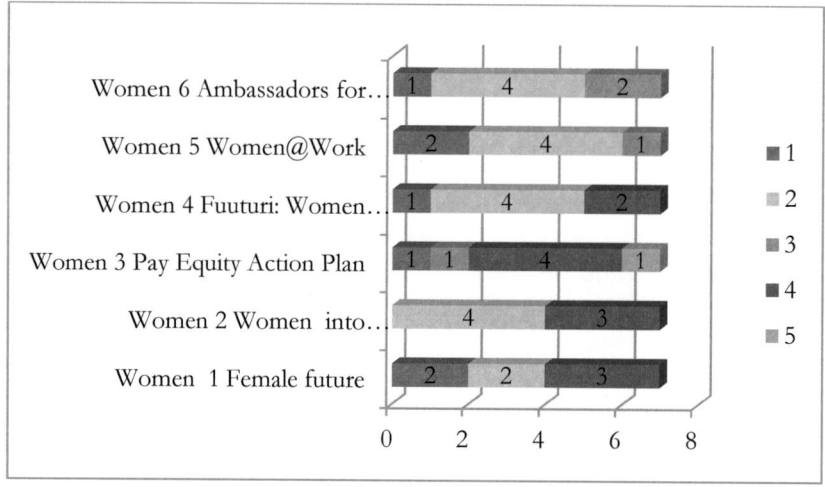

* 1- definitely disagree, 2- rather disagree, 3- I have no option, 4- rather agree, 5- definitely agree
Source: own work.

According to the respondents, the national and regional authorities have sufficient experience, knowledge and skills to implement the solutions proposed in the project (see Figure 31). However, some of the participants expressed concern that the initiators of implementing such solutions will not be receiving support from authorities (cf. Fig. 32).

Figure 31. In our country/region local government/institutions/partners do not have sufficient experience, skills and competences necessary for implementing this kind of practice – number of answers in total

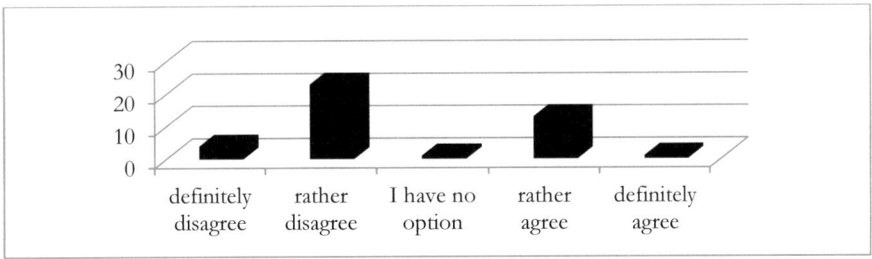

Source: own work.

Figure 32. In our country/region local government/institutions/partners cannot offer necessary support for other bodies that would implement this practice – number of answers in total

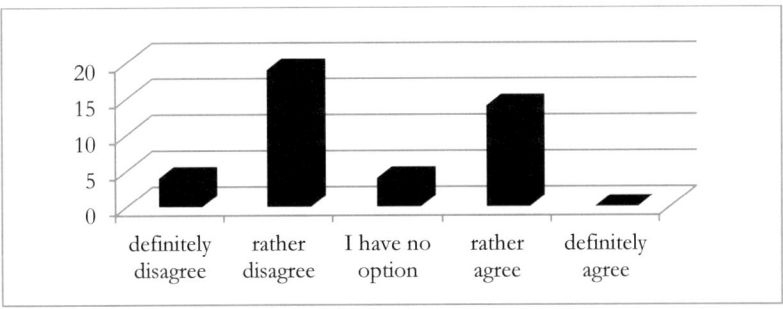

Source: own work.

Figure 33. In our country/region local government/institutions/partners cannot offer necessary support for other bodies that would implement this practice – number of answers in relation to each best practice*

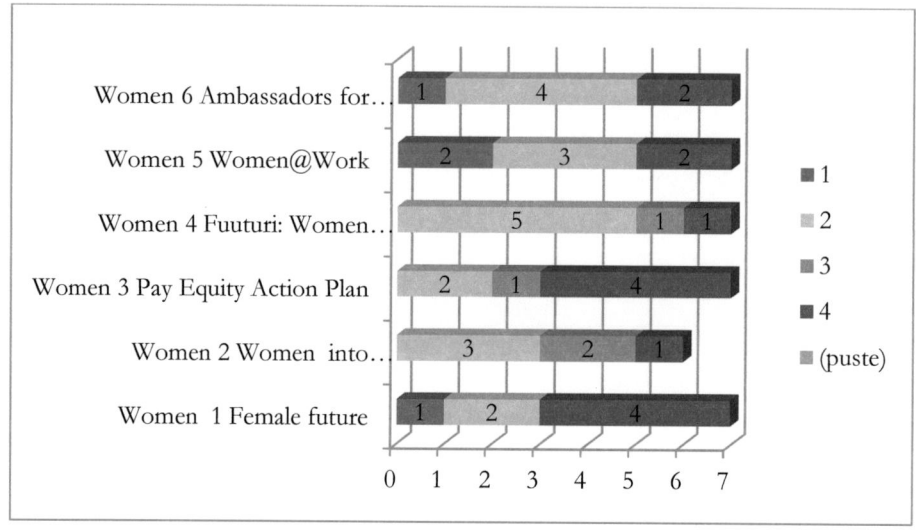

* 1- definitely disagree, 2- rather disagree, 3- I have no option, 4- rather agree, 5- definitely agree
Source: own work.

4.7. Formal and legal conditions for implementation of best practices related to the economic activity of women

Questions related to the formal and legal conditions for implementation of the proposed best practices yielded varied answers, which should encourage exercising greater caution in the process. On the one hand, most of the answers focused around the belief that in the respondents' countries of origin the rules allow for the implementation of the proposed solutions (see Fig. 34) and that such implementation would not require any additional licences or certifications (see Fig. 37) — on the other, however, many of them did not express any opinion on this matter or were convinced that there are no provision that would allow for the implementation of best practices. In addition, there were answers suggesting that existing rules are too inflexible (see Fig. 36). Due to formal and legal reasons, the greatest difficulties may be encountered when attempting to implement practice 3 (see Fig. 35).

Figure 34. In our country/region there are no regulations that allow for implementation of this project – number of answers in total

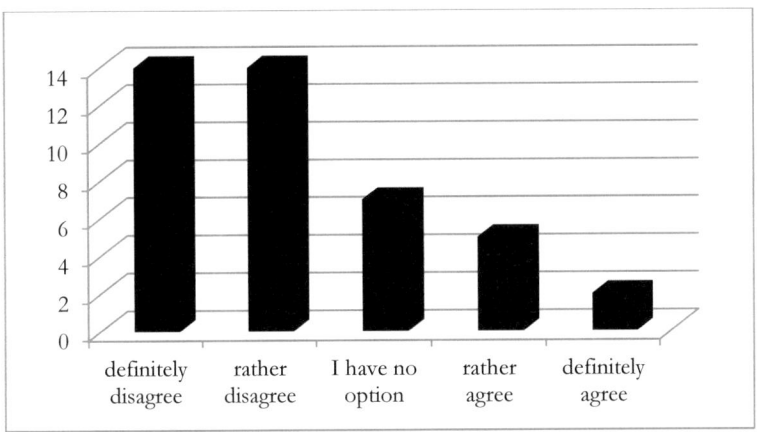

Source: own work.

Figure 35. In our country/region there are no regulations that allow for implementation of this project – number of answers in relation to each best practice*

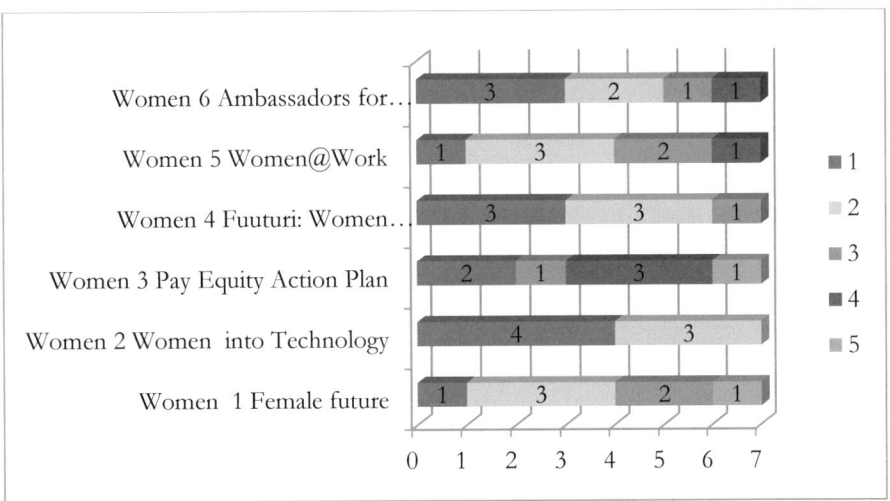

* 1- definitely disagree, 2- rather disagree, 3- I have no option, 4- rather agree, 5- definitely agree
Source: own work

Figure 36. In our country/region the regulations are not flexible enough and so do not allow to take into account particular actions and solutions that are a crucial element of this practice – number of answers in total

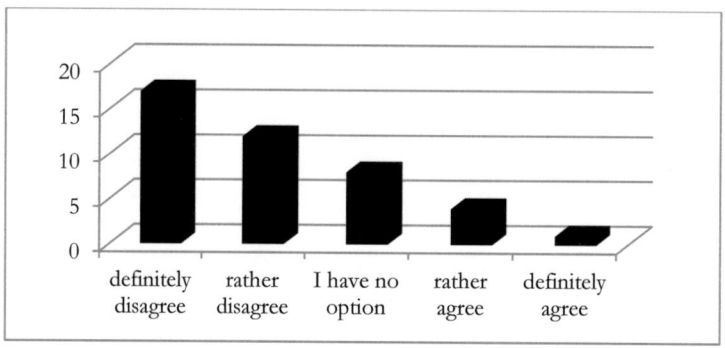

Source: own work.

Figure 37. Undertaking this practice requires additional permissions etc. by institutions implementing it – number of answers in total

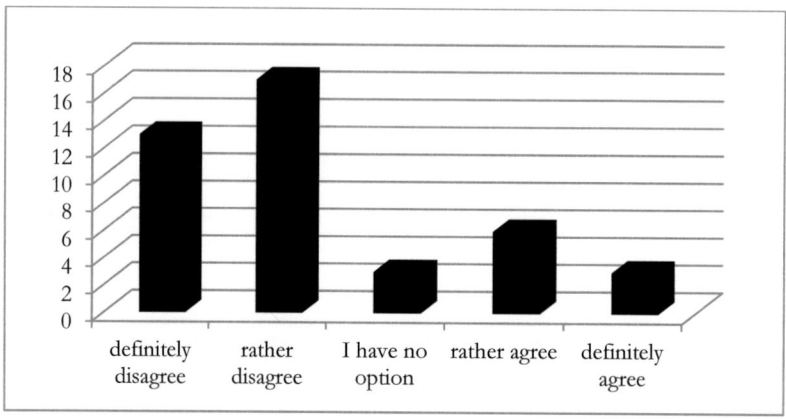

Source: own work.

4.8. Readiness and commitment of public and private partners in the process of implementing best practices related to the activation of women

In the last few years, the question of economic activation of women seems to be one of the main topics in the circle of issues related to the labour market. Hence, the majority of respondents answering the question about the consistency of the proposed best practices with the views accepted in the society indeed saw such coherence. However, there were also answers to the contrary. It seems that the need to change the consciousness with regard to the participation of excluded groups in the labour market may prove a serious issue in countries in which the implementation is to take place. Attention should be paid to the practices which arouse most controversy.

Figure 38. This practice is contradictory to traditional way of thinking and acting in our country/region in terms of integration of economically excluded groups into the labour market – number of answers in total

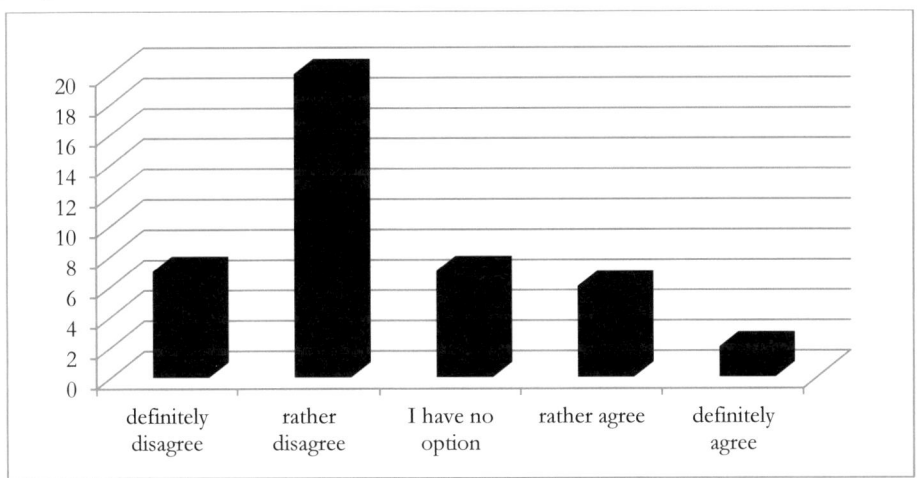

Source: own work.

Figure 39. This practice is contradictory to traditional way of thinking and acting in our country/region in terms of integration of economically excluded groups into the labour market – number of answers in relation to each best practice*

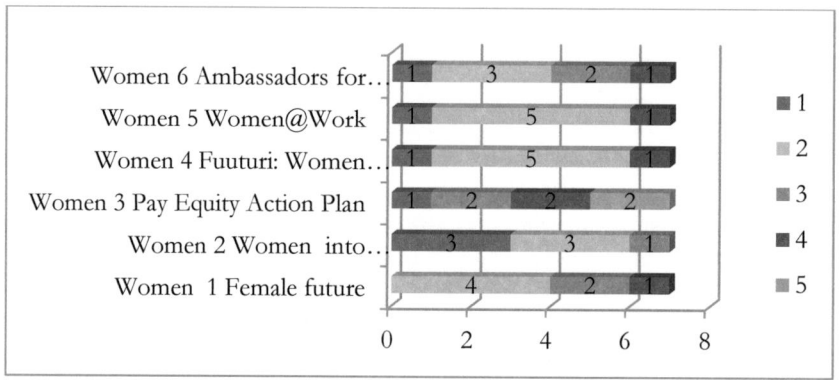

* 1- definitely disagree, 2- rather disagree, 3- I have no option, 4- rather agree, 5- definitely agree
Source: own work.

Most respondents claimed that their countries do not apply the solutions proposed as best practices (or that they are by no means widespread) (see Figure 42). Meanwhile, one of the main barriers can be the lack of motivation shown by the national and regional authorities or the social partners, leading to their failure to express interest in proposed solutions and involve in their implementation (see Figure 40). This is particularly evident in relation to practices 2 and 3 (see fig. 41).

Figure 40. In our country/region potential beneficiaries of such practice would not display sufficient motivation to participate in this practice /there are not enough incentives for participating in this practice – number of answers in total

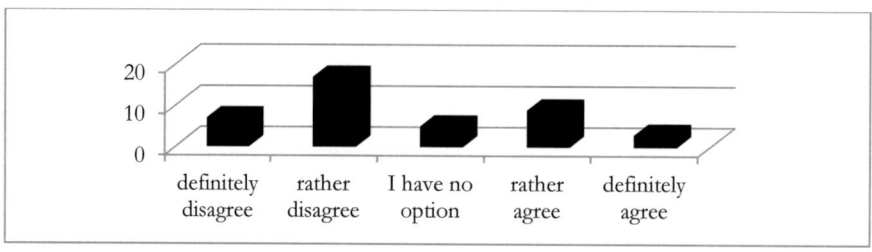

Source: own work.

Figure 41. In our country/region potential beneficiaries of such practice would not display sufficient motivation to participate in this practice /there are not enough incentives for participating in this practice – number of answers in relation to each best practice*

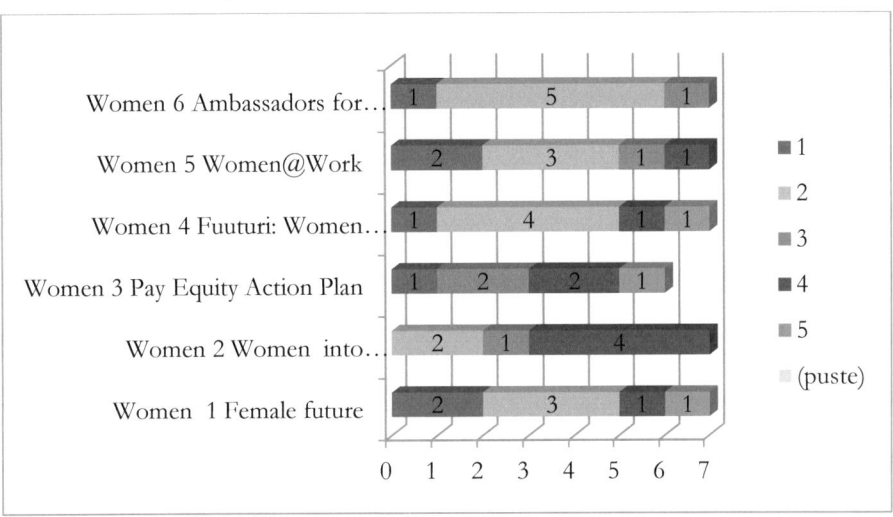

* 1- definitely disagree, 2- rather disagree, 3- I have no option, 4- rather agree, 5- definitely agree
Source: own work.

Figure 42. In our country/region there are already similar practices like this one and there is no need to implement this one – number of answers in total

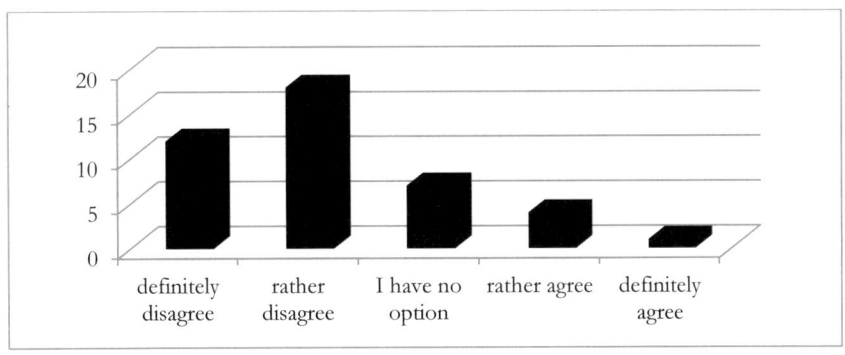

Source: own work.

5. Conclusions

In the analysis of the implementation conditions of selected best practices four categories were taken into account:

— financial issues, including the availability of aid from the European Union for the implementation of similar solutions,
— formal and legal issues,
— alignment of the best practice issues (economic activity of women and seniors in the context of developing innovation and competitiveness of SMEs) with the objectives and activities of the central, regional and local authorities and enterprises,
— readiness and commitment of public and private partners in the implementation process of the outlined best practices.

On the basis of the obtained answers it can be unequivocally stated that the risk of implementing any of the proposed solutions has been assessed as low (cf. Figures 43 and 45). In the case of best practices related to the economic activation of the seniors the practices recognized by respondents as burdened with high risk were "Senior enterprises – experience never ages" and "Senior policy in working life" (see Fig. 44), whereas in the case of practices oriented towards the activation of women the most risky are "Pay Equity Action Plan" and "Female Future" (see Figure 46).

Figure 43. The risk of failure for seniors' practices is high – number of answers in total

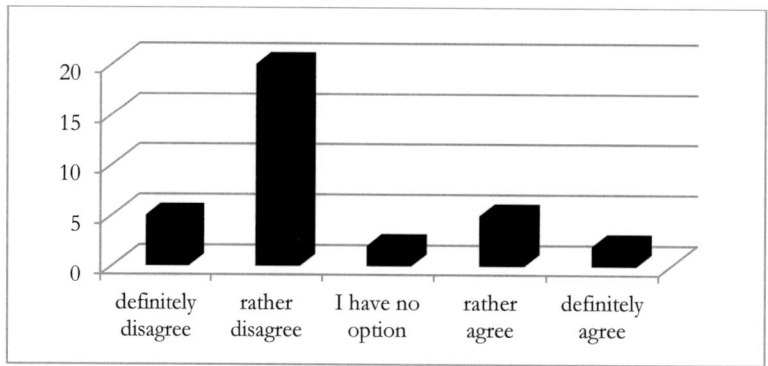

Source: own work.

Figure 44. The risk of failure for seniors' practices is high – number of answers in relation to each best practice*

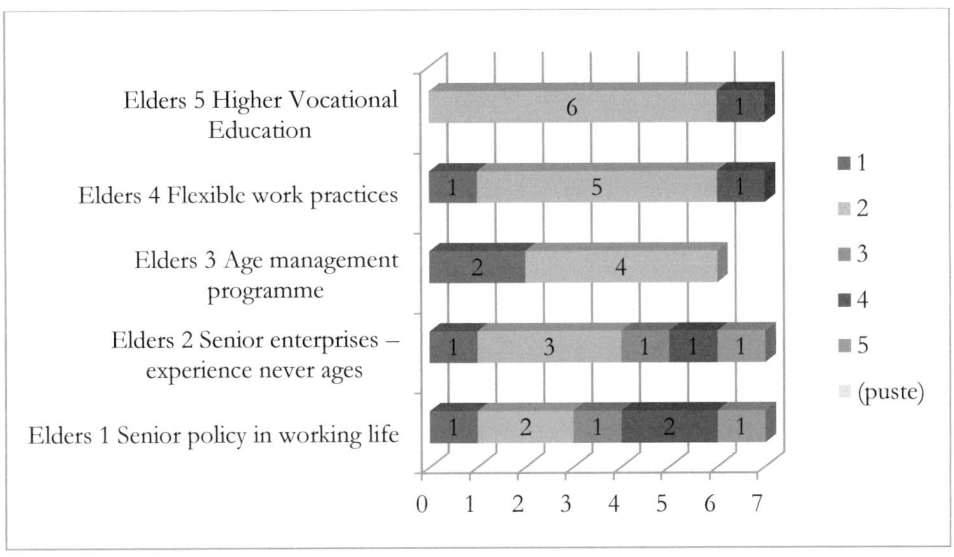

* 1- definitely disagree, 2- rather disagree, 3- I have no option, 4- rather agree, 5- definitely agree
Source: own work.

Figure 45. The risk of failure for women's practices is high – number of answers in total

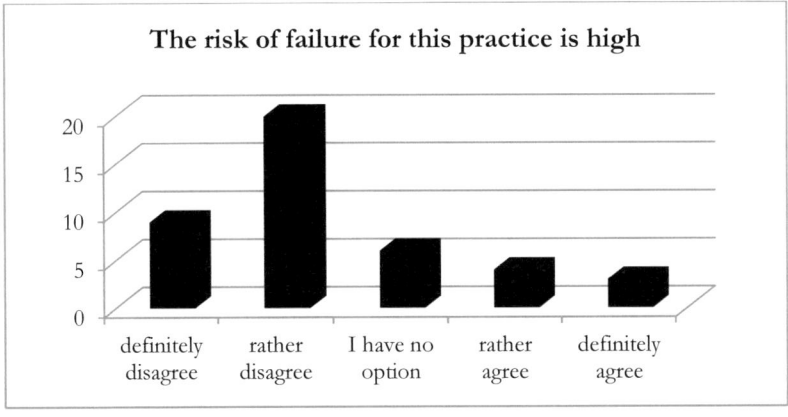

Source: own work.

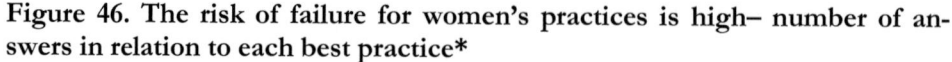

Figure 46. The risk of failure for women's practices is high– number of answers in relation to each best practice*

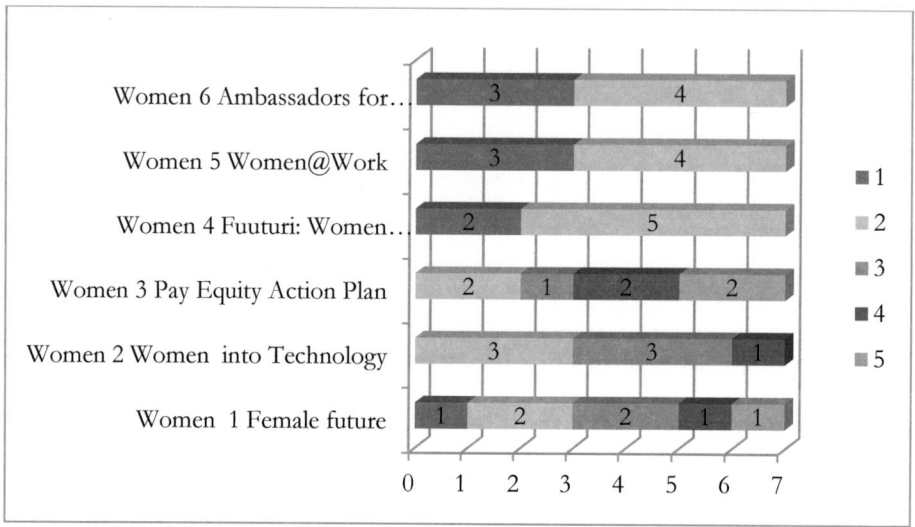

* 1- definitely disagree, 2- rather disagree, 3- I have no option, 4- rather agree, 5- definitely agree
Source: own work.

The results also allow for formulating some general conclusions:

— opportunities and conditions for the implementation of various best practices vary greatly due to their intrinsic characteristics,
— the efficiency of best practice implementation will be affected by the specificity of individual countries, and in particular by the level of public awareness — in this sense, the establishment of uniform guidelines regarding the implementation seems to be unfounded,
— one of the universal barriers (both in respect of the types of best practices and in respect of the country of implementation) is the shortage of own financial resources and low availability of external funds,
— a serious problem in the implementation of the proposed solutions may be related to the low public awareness of the need of economic activation of the groups hitherto traditionally marginalized in the labour market (mainly women and seniors), as well as to linking the activation to building innovation and competitiveness of enterprises — studies suggest that such awareness is low, although higher in the case of women,

— although the respondents assessed the implementation of the proposed best practices as relatively poor, they also said that the implementing entities will probably not be able to count on the support of national and regional authorities,
— a barrier to the authority engagement in the implementation process may be their lack of experience, knowledge and skills,
— the formal and legal issues should not be an obstacle to the implementation of the proposed best practices,
— **a key issue related to the implementation seems to be the low motivation of different types of entities to initiate the introduction of the proposed solutions.**

Part III The best practices transfer

1. The best practices transfer – practices improve women' activity

1.1. Female future mobilizing talents –a business perspective

Conditions of potential transfer of best practices from Norway to Germany

Enterprise, in which the best practices can be implemented

The project is so versatile that it can be implemented in both large, medium and small companies. The project can be implemented into both private and public companies and is targeted to businesses in all branches.

The best practices is aimed at all women, which are currently employed and want to develop their business knowledge.

The benefits of the transfer

Tangible, positive impact on women activity in the labour market and the efficiency growth of human resources in company. Removal of stereotypes about the role of women on the boards of companies in the society.

Benefits for enterprises: a better talent management, a better equipped workforces, more organizational learning. The practices brings fresh blood and new energy and enthusiasm into leadership of enterprise. The company also benefit from the enhanced reputation, with more female role models as a place for women to work.

The development in partnership between organization in the promotion process, specially a great opportunity for chambers capacity for women involvement.

Minimum requirements for transfer

The selection of companies, which are interested in the project are crucial. Enterprises must have money to cover women's participation in the training program. The choice of influential individuals (women and men) to be ambassadors and building a network of supportive ambassadors for the project is absolutely necessary for the effective implementation.

The finding of talented women in enterprise, which will be interested in the project is *a sine qua non for* the project.

Optimal conditions for the transfer

The condition greatly increasing the chances of the successful transfer of this practice is its promotion in the media. Additionally, the introduction of the best practices should be preceded by the expansive social campaign. It is because, in the case of transfer this practice to Germany, we should take into account cultural barriers. In Germany the mental barriers / gender stereotypes related with the acceptance women in management position are quite strong. In addition, in the German media rolls political debate about advantage and disadvantages on introduction "a female quota" (frauenquata).

What exactly, we should do, to make the transfer successful? Before starting this initiative, success stories in media more often about women who work at executive positions and materials for training women to gain real-life experience in real businesses should be published. The strong the advertising program among entrepreneurs about advantages of this program is necessary . Selection for the ambassadors persons with a warm positive public image is desired.

Generally, the success of implementation depends on the willingness of companies to support women in their professional career. Poor institutional childcare facilities only tell half the story in Germany, so companies must ensure a good balance between work and private life, to make this practice a successful story.

How, to measure the success to transfer? It should be measured by two aspects. We should use measures associated with membership (a number of ambassadors, a number of women involved in project) and measures associated with women members (women achievements, awards received by company/ women).

Conditions of potential transfer of best practices from Norway to Poland

Enterprise, in which the best practices can be implemented

The project can be implemented into both private and public companies and is targeted to businesses in all branches. The best practices is aimed at all women, which are currently employed and want to develop their business knowledge.

The project is so versatile that it can be implemented in both large, medium and small companies.

The benefits of the transfer

The positive impact on women activity in the labour market. The Polish economy is placed on the last position in UE, if we take in account the women activity rate on labor market, it is why the transfer is so beneficial for Polish economy. The practices can influence on the economic strength of region as a modern and friendly place for women to work.

Benefits for enterprises: a better talent management, a better equipped workforces, more organizational learning. The company also benefit from the enhanced reputation, with more female role models as a place for women to work.

The development in partnership between organization in the promotion process, specially a great opportunity for chambers capacity for women involvement.

Minimum requirements for transfer

The selection of companies, which are interested in the project are crucial. Enterprises must have money to cover women's participation in the training program. The choice of influential positive individuals (women and men) to be ambassadors and building a network of supportive ambassadors for the project is absolutely necessary for the effective implementation.

The finding of talented women in enterprise, which will be interested in the project is *a sine qua non for* the project.

Optimal conditions for the transfer

The practices requires form companies the ability to pay the costs relating to women participation in the Future Females program. This causes that most SME's can have problems, and even the inability to participate in the project. Therefore, it is indispensable to optimize a transfer by a wide access to information about potential, financial external sources for this kind of project. The project's implementing authority should provide the assistance in applying for EU funding, which allow greatly increase the chances of project transfer.

The big problem in implementation of this best practices is a lack among potential women of such project a sufficient motivation in the participation in program. It is why, it in necessary to show a individual success story of Norwegian women, who took part in FF program in Norway.

For the effective transfer of the practice to Poland, it would be important to choose a large, well-known women's organization as a leader in practice's implementation on the Polish market. It could be for example Polish Women Network. However, the coordinators at the local level, strengthening the transfer could be local organizations supporting entrepreneurship or chambers of commerce.

The condition, which allow to greatly increase the chances of successful transfer of this practice is the promotion of the best practices in the media. Additionally, the introduction of the best practices should be preceded by the expansive social campaign.

Conditions of potential transfer of best practices from Norway to Latvia

The addresses of the best practice

The project is targeted to businesses in all branches, to small, medium and large enterprises. The best practices is aimed at all women, which are currently employed and want to develop their business knowledge. In year 2012 the rate of women on boards in Latvia exceeds the EU-27 average (14%) and comprised 26%, rate of women in (executive) management positions exceed EU – 27 average (33%) and comprises

36%. So, despite the fact that the share of Latvian women in top management is quite high, there is a big demand among women in holistic training program that consists of personal leadership training, board competence and rhetoric.

The benefits of the transfer

Positive impact on women activity in the local labour market and regional development.

Benefits for enterprises: a better talent management, a better equipped workforces, more organizational learning. The company also benefit from the enhanced reputation, with more female role models as a place for women to work.

The development in partnership between organization in the promotion process, specially a great opportunity for chambers capacity for women involvement.

Minimum requirements for transfer

The selection of companies, which are interested in the project are crucial. Enterprises must have money to cover women's participation in the training program. The choice of influential positive individuals (women and men) to be ambassadors and building a network of supportive ambassadors for the project is absolutely necessary for the effective implementation.

The finding of talented women in enterprise, which will be interested in the project is *a sine qua non for* the project.

Optimal conditions for the transfer

The practice requires from companies the ability to pay the costs relating to women participation in the Future Females program. This causes that most SME's can have some problems, and even the inability to participate in the project. Therefore, it would be indispensable to optimize a transfer by a wide access to information about potential, financial external sources for this kind of project. The project's implementing authority should provide the assistance in applying for EU funding, which allow greatly to increase the chances of project transfer. But the best situation would be to raise funds by the organization implementing the project. The role (if the full funding will be possible) could play for example Latvian Employers Confederation or Latvian Chamber of Commerce and Industry. The necessity of making a complex formal application for external funding by all partners could discourage them.

The limitation of the effective implementation of this best practices on Latvian market can be the insufficient support from country/ regional/ local institutions. It is why, it could be fruitful to establish the cooperation between the Norwegian partner, who took part in FF program in Norway and Latvian organization.

The effective transfer of this practice to Latvia requires an intensive social campaign, because the majority of Latvian society is strongly against the" quota system". The aim of this promotion would be to present FF project as some alternative to "quota system", where women receive top management positions because of their skill, competence, experience and talents.

Conditions of potential transfer of best practices from Norway to Lithuania

The addresses of the best practice

The project is targeted to businesses in all branches, to small, medium and large enterprises. The best practices is aimed at all women, which are currently employed and want to develop their business knowledge. The practice is addressed to organizations, which support the activity of women in the labor market and which support the women entrepreneurship.

The benefits of the transfer

Positive impact on women activity in the local labour market and regional development.

Benefits for enterprises: a better talent management, a better equipped workforces, more organizational learning. The company also benefit from the enhanced reputation, with more female role models as a place for women to work.

The development in partnership between organization in the promotion process, specially a great opportunity for chambers capacity for women involvement.

Minimum requirements for transfer

The selection of companies, which are interested in the project are crucial. Enterprises must have money to cover women's participation in the training program. The choice of influential positive individuals (women and men) to be ambassadors and building a network of supportive ambassadors for the project is absolutely necessary for the effective implementation.

The finding of talented women in enterprise, which will be interested in the project is *a sine qua non for* the project.

Optimal conditions for the transfer

Organizing more broadminded trainings about women leadership, business management by women, various business-case analyses and workshops with business management situations to get relative experience before starting on a real-life initiative is highly recommended.

The practice requires from companies the ability to pay the costs relating to women participation in the Future Females program. This causes that most SME's can have some problems, and even the inability to participate in the project. Therefore, it would be indispensable to optimize a transfer by a wide access to information about potential, financial external sources for this kind of project. The project's implementing authority should provide the assistance in applying for EU funding, which allow greatly to increase the chances of project transfer. But the best situation would be to raise funds by the organization implementing the project. The necessity of making a complex formal application for external funding by all partners could discourage them to participate in project.

The limitation of the effective implementation of this best practices on Lithuanian market can be the insufficient support from country/ regional/ local institutions. It is why, it could be fruitful to establish the cooperation between the Norwegian partner, who took part in FF program in Norway and Lithuanian organization.

1.2. Women into technology

Conditions of potential transfer of best practices from Scotland to Germany

Actors of the best practices

The best practices is aimed at all women, which are currently unemployed, specially with low or no previous qualifications, who have been out of the labour market for long period.

The project is so versatile that it can be implemented in both large, medium and small companies. The project can be implemented into both private and public companies and is targeted to businesses in all branches.

The benefits of the transfer

Positive impact on women activity on the labour market. One of the largest problems related with the low participation of women in the labour market in the BSR countries is their under-representation in higher level ICT jobs. It is especially important, as the ICT sector is characterized by significant jobs growth dynamics.

Removal of stereotypes about the of women not working in "male" jobs (ICT, industry).

Benefits for enterprises: finding an employee, which training and skills are exactly in line with the expectations and needs of employers, a good reputation for company as a good place for women to work.

The development in partnership between local organization/ partners (enterprises, chambers, universities, business support institutions, government agencies)

Minimum requirements for transfer

The selection of actors, which are interested in creating the network is crucial. The network must include actors that are closely related to the ICT sector and the labor market.

The full financial support for implementing authority is a basic prerequisite for the effective implementation of practices.

Finding women, who will want to spend a weekend to study for a period of 48 weeks is a basic requirement for effective project implementation

Optimal conditions for the transfer

The promotion of this initiative in office job, portals providing information on obtaining a job or upgrade skills, organizations supporting female entrepreneurship is very desirable. Because of the risk, that such practice would not display sufficient motivation to participate in this practice (there could be not enough incentives for participating in this practice), it is necessary to distribute in media the positive examples where similar programes have worked very well.

To optimalize the practice's transfer is important to provide a better and more inclusive working environment for women. Women, who will take part in this project should have a supportive atmosphere connected with a high standard of training. Because the program is aimed mainly at unemployed women, it would desirable to cover travel and childcare costs during the weekend, the cost of the purchase of books or exams fees.

Also, a strong local support and collaboration between universities, firms and local authorities is highly recommended. Chambers and other institutions, which represent the interest of local firms would have to acknowledge the economic advantages of women training in ICT sector.

Conditions of potential transfer of best practices from Scotland to Poland

Actors of the best practices

The best practices is aimed at all women, which are currently unemployed, specially with low or no previous qualifications, who have been out of the labour market for long period.

The project is so versatile that it can be implemented in both large, medium and small companies. The project can be implemented into both private and public companies and is targeted to businesses in all branches.

The benefits of the transfer

Positive impact on women activity on the labour market. One of the largest problems related with the low participation of women in the labour market in the BSR countries is their under-representation in higher level ICT jobs. It is especially important, as the ICT sector is characterized by significant jobs growth dynamics.

Removal of stereotypes about the of women not working in "male" jobs (ICT, industry).

Benefits for enterprises: finding an employee, which training and skills are exactly in line with the expectations and needs of employers, a good reputation for company as a good place for women to work.

The development in partnership between local organization/ partners (enterprises, chambers, universities, business support institutions, government agencies)

Minimum requirements for transfer

The selection of actors, which are interested in creating the network is crucial. The network must include actors that are closely related to the ICT sector and the labor market.

The full financial support for implementing authority is a basic prerequisite for the effective implementation of practices.

Finding women, who will want to spend a weekend to study for a period of 48 weeks is a basic requirement for effective project implementation

Optimal conditions for the transfer

Because of very little own sources among institutions potentially interested in implementing this kind of solution in Poland, the applying for EU funding is highly recommended.

The social campaign in media for breaking stereotypes and encourage women to study IT is also very desirable. The promotion of this initiative in office job, portals providing information on obtaining a job or upgrade skills, organizations supporting female entrepreneurship is very desirable. Because of the risk, that such practice would not display sufficient motivation to participate in this practice (there could be not enough incentives for participating in this practice), it is necessary to distribute in media the positive examples where similar programmes have worked very well.

To optimalize the practice's transfer is important to provide a better and more inclusive working environment for women. Women, who will take part in this project should have a supportive atmosphere connected with a high standard of training. Because the program is aimed mainly at unemployed women, it would desirable to cover travel and childcare costs during the weekend, the cost of the purchase of books or exams fees.

Also, a strong local support and collaboration between universities, firms and local authorities is highly recommended. Chambers and other institutions, which represent the interest of local firms would have to acknowledge the economic advantages of women training in ICT sector.

Conditions of potential transfer of best practices from Scotland to Lithuania

The addressees of the initiative

At first programme was aimed at long term unemployed women, at lonely parents, black and minority ethnic women, and women with disabilities.

This initiatives, on a higher level, should be taken by local bodies such as chambers, local employers, local authorities, local training agencies to have a programme designed to local market needs.

Benefits of the practice transfer

Individual personal development of participant women.

Increase in knowledge and use of relevant ICT skills adequate to current job situation in the region among women.

Good reading of local job market needs.

Integrated support to training process of women– not only the sole training, training materials are provided but also travelling and childcare expenses are covered

Increase in women employment in ICT related/linked jobs.

Activities to be undertaken to transfer the practice

Identification of local training centres that could undertake the activity.

Creating good local partners' network.

Reading of local market needs – the training programme might vary depending on the location.

Identification of professional training organization experienced in providing training services to disadvantaged groups.

Minimal requirements for the transfer

Additional funding programme, directed towards equal opportunities would be conducive for finding relevant, at least partial external funding of the initiative.

Recruitment of women participants that will manage to attend the course in such long time.

Self-selection of volunteer training centres to implement this kind of initiative.

Optimal conditions for the transfer

Building community awareness (especially women) about future possibilities in ICT sphere.

Adding value elements of the programme as described earlier – returns on travel expenses, childcare provision or childcare cost returns.

Promotion of the initiative in wider business-local authorities-NGOs environments.

Linking the programme with any wider policy actions aimed at breaking gender stereotypes.

Conditions of potential transfer of best practices from Scotland to Latvia

The addressees of the initiative

At first programme was aimed at long term unemployed women, at lonely parents, black and minority ethnic women, and women with disabilities.

This initiatives, on a higher level, should be taken by local bodies such as chambers, local employers, local authorities, local training agencies to have a programme designed to local market needs.

Benefits of the practice transfer (for addressees and region)

Individual personal development of participant women.

Increase in knowledge and use of relevant ICT skills adequate to current job situation in the region among women.

Good reading of local job market needs.

Integrated support to training process of women– not only the sole training, training materials are provided but also travelling and childcare expenses are covered

Increase in women employment in ICT related/linked jobs.

Activities to be undertaken to transfer the practice

Identification of local training centres that could undertake the activity.

Creating good local partners' network.

Reading of local market needs – the training programme might vary depending on the location.

Identification of professional training organization experienced in providing training services to disadvantaged groups.

Minimal requirements for the transfer

Additional funding programme, directed towards equal opportunities would be conducive for finding relevant, at least partial external funding of the initiative.

Recruitment of women participants that will manage to attend the course in such long time.

Self-selection of volunteer training centres to implement this kind of initiative.

Optimal conditions for the transfer

Building community awareness (especially women) about future possibilities in ICT sphere.

Adding value elements of the programme as described earlier – returns on travel expenses, childcare provision or childcare cost returns.

Promotion of the initiative in wider business-local authorities-NGOs environments.

Linking the programme with any wider policy actions aimed at breaking gender stereotypes.

1.3. Fuuturi: Women entrepreneurs and managers in the future

Conditions of potential transfer of best practices from Finland to Germany

The addressees of the initiative

Women entrepreneurs and managers working on their business development and internationalization, also pursuing own development projects. Also, it involved women employees and managers.

This initiative should be undertaken by local chambers, existing networks of women as well as local governmental bodies.

The benefits of the transfer

Activation of local existing networks of women in different locations (sparsely populated in particular) and so no need to start other networks. Good activation of networks in chambers. Great opportunity for using chambers' capacity for women involvement.

Study visits in businesses and organizations increase knowledge of participants but also raise awareness on gender issues and so are breaking gender stereotypes among a variety of stakeholders.

Raising number of growing businesses in sparsely populated areas. Strengthening local economies. Also internationalizing local businesses.

Raising trust and community building process.

Increasing self-efficacy of women via promoting can-do attitude.

Building and developing advantages and actions among women entrepreneurs, managers and employees.

Strengthening contacts between coaches and participants. This might serve as a seedpoint for further development of networks.

Activities to be undertaken to transfer the practice

A number of evenly distributed locations across a region or a country should be identified. Existing strong professional networks, chambers in different areas should be identified as well as existing circles and networks of women (not necessarily acting in business) should be approached.

The promotion among women in sparsely populated areas should take place on a very local level (libraries, local shops) and some incentives should be given. The promotion should also be actively made in venues where women entrepreneurs come for administrative purposes. It is important to involve women employees too.

The incorporation of e-business module seems important as it proved successful and useful in North Savonia for female entrepreneurs

Courses and trainings should be tailor made therefore, the design of training programme needs to be a response to actual needs and suggestions expressed by women.

Minimal requirements for the transfer

This initiative requires recruitment of participants who can afford payment for the training and coaching programme. Appropriate fee needs to be set so that it was not too high.

Participant groups need to be well-defined beforehand (existing entrepreneurs or existing plus future entrepreneurs)

A number of key local leaders need to be identified to promote the initiative.

Coach who asks questions and does not give ready solutions, not traditional consultant.

Some non-pecuniary support such as the base for networking opportunities and help with work-life balance should be clearly promoted as it is highly appreciated among German women

Optimal conditions for the transfer

Promotion of initiative in local environments.

The engagement of different actors in local communities, actors from entrepreneurship support system.

Existing initiatives (women networks or similar) may be taken advantage in terms of participant recruitment, coach recruitment, for the sake of strengthening existing networks. These do not have to be directly focused on internationalization, existing project development but respond to dominant concerns of enterprises.

Dissemination of practice will not only ease up start up and business development processes but also will break gender stereotypes in terms of women economic activity.

Conditions of potential transfer of best practices from Finland to Poland

The addressees of the initiative

Women entrepreneurs and managers working on their business development and internationalization, also pursuing own development projects. Also, it involved women employees and managers.

This initiative should be undertaken by local chambers, existing networks of women as well as local governmental bodies.

Benefits of the practice transfer (for addressees and region)

Activation of local existing networks of women in different locations (sparsely populated in particular) and so no need to start other networks. Good activation of networks in chambers, especially women networks. Great opportunity for using chambers' capacity for women involvement.

Study visits in businesses and organizations increase knowledge of participants but also raise awareness on gender issues and so are breaking gender stereotypes among a variety of stakeholders.

Raising number of growing businesses in sparsely populated areas. Strengthening local economies. Also internationalizing local businesses.

Raising trust and community building process.

Increasing self-efficacy of women via promoting can-do attitude.

Building and developing advantages and actions among women entrepreneurs, managers and employees.

Strengthening contacts between coaches and participants. This might serve as a seedpoint for further development of networks

Activities to be undertaken to transfer the practice

A number of evenly distributed locations across a region or a country could be identified. Existing strong professional networks, chambers in different areas should be identified as well as existing circles and networks of women (not necessarily acting in business) should be approached. In Poland, there are still few women networks, and this initiative can use even such a small capacity.

The promotion among women in sparsely populated areas should take place on a very local level (libraries, local shops) and some incentives should be given. The promotion should also be actively made in venues where women entrepreneurs come for administrative purposes. It is important to involve women employees too.

The incorporation of e-business module seems important as it proved successful and useful in North Savonia for female entrepreneurs

Courses and trainings should be tailor made therefore, the design of training programme needs to be a response to actual needs and suggestions expressed by women.

Minimal requirements for the transfer

This initiative requires recruitment of participants who can afford payment for the training and coaching programme. Appropriate fee needs to be set so that it was not too high.

Participant groups need to be well-defined beforehand (existing entrepreneurs or existing plus future entrepreneurs)

A number of key local leaders should to be identified to promote the initiative.

Some non-financial support such as the base for networking opportunities and help with work-life balance as it is very rare and uncommon in Poland. Some childcare could be provided for the time of training.

Optimal conditions for the transfer

Promotion of initiative in local environments.

The engagement of different actors in local communities, actors from entrepreneurship support system.

Existing initiatives (women networks or similar) may be taken advantage in terms of participant recruitment, coach recruitment, for the sake of strengthening existing networks. These do not have to be directly focused on internationalization, existing project development but respond to dominant concerns of enterprises.

Promoting additional support – such as childcare onplace of training and meetings - participants receive. This might attract media attention as such practices are not very common.

Dissemination of practice will not only ease up start up and business development processes but also will break gender stereotypes in terms of women economic activity.

Conditions of potential transfer of best practices from Finland to Lithuania

The addressees of the initiative

Women entrepreneurs and managers working on their business development and internationalization, also pursuing own development projects. Also, it involved women employees and managers.

This initiative should be undertaken by local chambers, existing networks of women as well as local governmental bodies.

Benefits of the practice transfer (for addressees and region)

Activation of local existing networks of women in different locations (sparsely populated in particular) and so no need to start other networks. Potential activation of networks in chambers. Great opportunity for using chambers' capacity for women involvement.

Study visits in businesses and organizations increase knowledge of participants but also raise awareness on gender issues and so are breaking gender stereotypes among a variety of stakeholders.

Raising number of growing businesses in sparsely populated areas. Strengthening local economies. Also internationalizing local businesses.

Raising trust and community building process.

Increasing self-efficacy of women via promoting can-do attitude.

Building and developing advantages and actions among women entrepreneurs, managers and employees.

Strengthening contacts between coaches and participants. This might serve as a seedpoint for further development of networks

Activities to be undertaken to transfer the practice

A number of evenly distributed locations across a region or a country should be identified. Existing strong professional networks, chambers in different areas should be identified as well as existing circles and networks of women (not necessarily acting in business) should be approached.

The promotion among women in sparsely populated areas should take place on a very local level (libraries, local shops) and some incentives should be given. The promotion should also be actively made in venues where women entrepreneurs come for administrative purposes. It is important to involve women employees too.

The incorporation of e-business module seems important as it proved successful and useful in North Savonia for female entrepreneurs

Minimal requirements for the transfer

This initiative requires recruitment of participants who can afford payment for the training and coaching programme. Appropriate fee needs to be set so that it was not too high.

Participant groups need to be well-defined beforehand (existing entrepreneurs or existing plus future entrepreneurs)

A number of key local leaders need to be identified to promote the initiative.

Coach who asks questions and does not give ready solutions, not traditional consultant.

Optimal conditions for the transfer

Promotion of initiative in local environments.

The engagement of different actors in local communities, actors from entrepreneurship support system.

Existing initiatives (women networks or similar) may be taken advantage in terms of participant recruitment, coach recruitment, for the sake of strengthening existing networks.

Support to find funding (crowdfunding) for women start-ups would be essential for the women to be interested in taking part in the initiative

Increasing media attention and organizing public events, i.e. seminars, workshops about entrepreneurship for women.

Projects can be focused on internationalization, existing project development but also respond to dominant concerns of enterprises.

Dissemination of practice will not only ease up start up and business development processes but also will break gender stereotypes in terms of women economic activity.

Conditions of potential transfer of best practices from Finland to Latvia

The addressees of the initiative

Women entrepreneurs and managers working on their business development and internationalization, also pursuing own development projects. Also, it involved women employees and managers.

This initiative should be undertaken by local chambers, existing networks of women as well as local governmental bodies.

Benefits of the practice transfer (for addressees and region)

Activation of local existing networks of women in different locations (sparsely populated in particular) and so no need to start other networks. Good activation of networks in chambers. Great opportunity for using chambers' capacity for women involvement.

Study visits in businesses and organizations increase knowledge of participants but also raise awareness on gender issues and so are breaking gender stereotypes among a variety of stakeholders.

Raising number of growing businesses in sparsely populated areas. Strengthening local economies. Also internationalizing local businesses.

Raising trust and community building process.

Increasing self-efficacy of women via promoting can-do attitude.

Building and developing advantages and actions among women entrepreneurs, managers and employees.

Strengthening contacts between coaches and participants. This might serve as a seedpoint for further development of networks

Activities to be undertaken to transfer the practice

A number of evenly distributed locations across a region or a country should be identified. Existing strong professional networks, chambers in different areas should be identified as well as existing circles and networks of women (not necessarily acting in business) should be approached.

The promotion among women in sparsely populated areas should take place on a very local level (libraries, local shops) and some incentives should be given. The promotion should also be actively made in venues where women entrepreneurs come for administrative purposes. It is important to involve women employees too.

The incorporation of e-business module seems important as it proved successful and useful in North Savonia for female entrepreneurs

Minimal requirements for the transfer

This initiative requires recruitment of participants who can afford payment for the training and coaching programme. Appropriate fee needs to be set so that it was not too high.

Participant groups need to be well-defined beforehand (existing entrepreneurs or existing plus future entrepreneurs)

A number of key local leaders need to be identified to promote the initiative.

As the aim is to develop new potentials of the existing companies or acquire new markets. This is quite new angle that might be interesting to Latvia as well. Currently Latvia motivates entrepreneurs focus more on export markets not only on Latvia market itself. Companies are lacking knowledge how to develop new products and how to enter new markets.

EU funding can be necessary. This action can be implemented in cooperation with Latvian Development Agency in order to find new potential markets for the products and services of the companies.

Optimal conditions for the transfer

Promotion of initiative in local environments.

The engagement of different actors in local communities, actors from entrepreneurship support system.

Existing initiatives (women networks or similar) may be taken advantage in terms of participant recruitment, coach recruitment, for the sake of strengthening existing networks. These can be focused on internationalization, existing project development but also respond to dominant concerns of enterprises.

Dissemination of practice will not only ease up start up and business development processes but also will break gender stereotypes in terms of women economic activity.

1.4. Pay Equity Action Plan

Conditions of potential transfer of best practices from Sweden to Germany

Enterprise, in which the best practices can be implemented

The project can be implemented in both large, medium and small companies. The original best practice covers the male and female employees in enterprises with 10 or more employees. The project can be implemented into both private and public companies and is targeted to businesses in all branches.

The benefits of the transfer

There are numerous benefits of implementing a pay equity plan, specially for employees and employers. The positive work atmosphere is the first and most important benefit for all. For employers the transfer of this practice means the reduction of costs associated with attracting, retaining, and motivating skilled workforce. By implementing this practice, the employers will have a bank of accurate up-to-date job descriptions, clearly defined criteria for hiring employees and a good formalized salary administration system.

Each company by implementing this practice is building the image of a socially responsible entity, because pay equity is a fundamental human right.

Activities to be undertaken to transfer the practice

First of all, legal possibilities of the Equality Action Plan's implementation should be checked.

The final shape of the Plan should be consulted among enterprise's organizations, chambers of trade, chambers of handcraft, employee's organizations.

Minimum requirements for transfer

The conviction of enterprises to join the project is crucial. Each year, employers will be required to carry out a paid survey and analyze their pay policies and practices, even in cases when no disparity was identified in the previous year. So enterprises must have money to do a high quality research on pay gaps. To measure the results of introduction of "pay equality action plan", the evaluation of surveys should be carried by one selected national organization. The choice and the engagement of this institution is a crucial factor of successful transfer.

Optimal conditions for the transfer

The condition greatly increasing the chances of the successful transfer of this practice is its promotion in the media. In this campaign the clear strategy on the government level, showing what a government have just done in this area (e.g. in Germany free Excel tool that helps firms to calculate the firm-specific gender specific wage gap named LOGIB-D) and what will do (e.g. the implementation of Pay Equity Action Plan in 50% public enterprises in the next 5 years) should be indicated. We recommend the collaboration between employees and employer's representatives on the pay equity process from the beginning of the planning stage. This will help ensure the process is open and honest, and that its results are acceptable.

Generally, the success of implementation depends on amenities, created by the implementing institution. This institution should create a job comparison system, adapted to all enterprises using an interactive PDF form. This tool should contain drop-down menus and step-by-step instructions for creating a system, into which one can enter job information and compare jobs. It would be very useful to clarify the competence of evaluation institution, show which exactly services it can offer to enterprises and what enterprises have to do for the institution.

How, to measure the success of transfer? It could be measured by two indices: number of all enterprises, which implemented Pay Equity Action Plan or/ and by SME's number, which joined the Action Plan..

Conditions of potential transfer of best practices from Sweden to Poland

Enterprise, in which the best practices can be implemented

The project can be implemented in large, medium and small companies. The original best practice covers the male and female employees in enterprises with 10 or more employees. The project can be implemented into both private and public companies and is targeted to businesses in all branches.

The benefits of the transfer

The benefits for employer are: an increase of retention and reduction of staff turnover, a strength of recruitment efforts, a lower absenteeism, an improvement of workplace morale, a higher security of stable workforce, a solution of workplace skills/needs shortages. These benefits can lead to growth of the workplace productivity.

Employee benefits include: an increased levels of job satisfaction, an improved employee health and well-being, the increased level of engagement at the workplace, a decreased work-related stress, the increased sharing of family responsibility, an improved work-life balance, a wider career diversity for women.

In each economy, pay and employment equity practices improve the supply and the skill level of labour. Broader recruitment tools and pay equality employment practices unaffected by gender can upgrade workforce quality and productivity.

Activities to be undertaken to transfer the practice

First of all, legal possibilities of the Equality Action Plan's implementation should be checked.

The final shape of the Plan should be consulted among enterprise's organizations, chambers of trade, chambers of handcraft, employee's organizations.

Minimum requirements for transfer

.The conviction of enterprises to join the project is crucial. Each year, employers will be required to carry out a paid survey and analyze their pay policies and practices, even in cases when no disparity was identified in the previous year. So enterprises must have money to do a high quality research on pay gaps. To measure the results of introduction of "pay equality action plan", the evaluation of surveys should be carried by one selected national organization (evaluation institution). The choice and the engagement of this institution is a crucial factor of successful transfer.

Optimal conditions for the transfer

The government can make many steps to increase changes of successful transfers of this practice. The government should promote a pay equity practices: promote business cases and employer tools, promote gender-based analysis in policies and projects, achieve a high quantity of "pay equity plan" implementations in public entities. The government can provide scholarships and mentorship for students, women and men, entering non-traditional training programs, which can help in transfer of this practice.

Employers can familiarize themselves with the new set of attitudes, participate in wage gap training and in public education campaign initiatives. In each company, it would be useful to establish a representative job evaluation committee that includes the employer, union and employee members to guide the pay equity process. This will help provide balanced perspectives and increase the credibility of the results.

It would be very useful to clarify the competence of evaluation institution, show which exactly services it can offer to enterprises and what enterprises have to do for the institution. It is very important, because the quality of an implemented "pay equality program" in enterprises can be very different. The implemented program may often not clearly explain the nature of the obligations of employers, nor the consequences of their non-compliance, could not provide adequate instructions with respect to acceptable standards and methods to establish pay equity.

Conditions of potential transfer of best practices from Sweden to Latvia

Enterprise, in which the best practices can be implemented

The project is can be implemented in both large, medium and small companies. The project can be implemented into both private and public companies and is targeted to businesses in all branches.

The benefits of the transfer

For economy this practice has tangible, positive impact on women activity in the labour market and on the growth of human resources. Transfer of this practice could improve the productivity and competitiveness of Latvian business through the advancement of gender equality in employment and in the workplace.

For employers, the introduction of this practice can bring the improvement of employees' morale, reduction of workforce turnover and increasing the ability to predict wage costs. In long term company could have simply a better equipped and satisfied workforce. The company can also benefit from enhanced reputation, as a place for women to work. This practice fosters workplace consultation between employers and employees on issues concerning gender equality in employment and in the workplace.

The practices bring fresh blood, new energy and enthusiasm among employees (specially women).

Activities to be undertaken to transfer the practice

First of all, legal possibilities of the Equality Action Plan's implementation should be checked The final shape of the Plan should be consulted among enterprise's organizations, chambers of trade, chambers of handcraft, employee's organizations.

.Minimum requirements for transfer

The conviction of enterprises to join the project is crucial. Each year, employers will be required to carry out a paid survey and analyze their pay policies and practices, even in cases when no disparity was identified in the previous year. So enterprises must have money to do a high quality research on pay gaps. To measure the results of introduction of "pay equality action plan", the evaluation of surveys should be carried by one selected national organization. The choice and the engagement of this institution is a crucial factor of successful transfer.

Optimal conditions for the transfer

In each company it would be recommended to establish a representative job evaluation committee that includes the employer, the union and employee members to guide the pay equity process. This will help provide balanced perspectives and increase the credibility of the results. Employers should be encouraged to implement a pay equity plan using a project management approach.

Probably the level of precision in employers' plans for equal play will be extremely varied. The contents of "Pay Equity Action Plan", where that salary adjustment will be carried out without cost calculation, is not acceptable. It is why, the evaluation institution should provide consultation and advisory services in relation to the development and implementation of pay equality action plan . With view to helping SME to meet the requirements of "Pay Equity Action Plan", evaluation institution has to prepare materials to guide SME's in the implementations of pay equality plan. It would be very useful to clarify the competence of evaluation institution, show which exactly services it can offer to enterprises and what enterprises have to do for the institution.

Government's social company based on demonstrating good faith, natural justice, human rights, advantages of practices' implementation would be very desirable. The government should encourage public sector organizations to joint voluntary the "Pay Equity Action Plan.

Conditions of potential transfer of best practices from Sweden to Lithuania

Enterprise, in which the best practices can be implemented

The project is can be implemented in both large, medium and small companies. The project can be implemented into private and public companies and is targeted to businesses in all branches.

The benefits of the transfer

This transfer can cause increasing labour force participation of women in each economy, which helps meet shortages of labour and skills and contributes to economic growth. Improved workforce participation of women generates a better level of return on the investment in women's education. This practice brings greater economic independence for women, reduce reliance on income support, and improve lifetime earnings and to tax. It improves women's capacity to contribute to pay off student loans earlier.

Due to implementation of this practice employees, are more committed to the organization, work harder, show more initiative and are more productive. For employers the transfer of this practice means the reduction of workforce turnover, an improvement of workplace morale and a quicker solution of workplace skills/needs shortages

Activities to be undertaken to transfer the practice

First of all, legal possibilities of the Equality Action Plan's implementation should be checked.

The final shape of the Plan should be consulted among enterprise's organizations, chambers of trade, chambers of handcraft, employee's organizations.

Minimum requirements for transfer

The conviction of enterprises to join the project is crucial. Each year, employers will be required to carry out a paid survey and analyze their pay policies and practices, even in cases when no disparity was identified in the previous year. So enterprises must have money to do a high quality research on pay gaps. To measure the results of introduction of "pay equality action plan", the evaluation of surveys should be carried by one selected national organization. The choice and the engagement of this institution is a crucial factor of successful transfer.

Optimal conditions for the transfer

Wide public awareness raising campaigns are needed in order to explain, why the introduction of this practice is necessary and what benefit will the employer gain by executing them. Public campaign, showing the existing differences in wages between men and women is also desirable.

Lithuanian governmental programme for years 2010-2014 of equality for women and men (Geco – sexual equality competence in business and research) does not oblige enterprises to execute annual surveys on payment gaps and to elaborate any action plans to promote gender equality. If such practice is implemented as a mandatory practice, it will be faced with anger and fulfilled formally. The better way is to create a system of incentives for enterprises to participate in project.

The role of national implementing institution is very important. It should prepare documents with basic information about a pay equity and some of its key concepts, such as wages and occupational groups, details of the four factors used in job comparisons: skill, effort, responsibility and working conditions. It should also get suggestions for evaluating the value of jobs. This guide should also include frequently asked questions.

How to measure the success to transfer? It could be measured by two indices : number of all enterprises, which implemented Pay Equity Action Plan or/ and by SME's number, which joined the Action Plan.

1.5. Women@Work

Conditions of potential transfer of best practices from United Kingdom to Germany

Actors of the best practices

The addresses are women. It focuses on those women living in rural areas, low paid women, ethnic minority women and young women (less than 30).

The benefits of the transfer

Participants to the organization and non-members can benefit in variety of ways. First: particular skills are developed via learning programs. Second: gives women more ability express their concerns in their local environments about gender issues. Also, it works as a forum for ideas and opinions exchange, creates broad networking opportunities via meetings, guest speeches and trainings.

Also, it involves women living in the rural areas in the skill development and raises their awareness on gender issues. It strengthens their economic and social presence in communities. This, is particularly relevant in regions with rural areas where women participation in civic and economic life is not sufficient.

Activities to be undertaken to transfer the practice

Existing networks, chambers in different areas could be identified as well as existing circles and networks of women (not necessarily acting in business) should be approached.

The promotion among women in sparsely populated areas should take place on a very local level (libraries, local shops) and some incentives could be given. The promotion should also be actively made in venues where women entrepreneurs come for administrative purposes.

Minimum requirements for transfer

Selecting organizations and recruiting key people who could combine the existing network resources and attract new organizations and actors. The network should include actors embedded in the rural communities.

Making the initiative not as another one, but a flagship, for example, promoted by local government.

The financial support is an important prerequisite for attracting and implementing the practice.

Optimal conditions for the transfer

The learning program should be locally adjusted by individual networks to the needs of women in their communities and the resources of the whole initiatives can be employed to cover the scope and diversity of needs and problems.

An active and up-to-date website portal with events, activities, blog, names and contact details of all the local chapters should be created.

The involvement of different, existing networks and NGOS will add to the promotion and dissemination of the initiative, it will also help to avoid doubling the activities and actions aimed at particular communities.

A strong management and start-up centre with staff recognizing the gender related challenges at a local and global level.

Such networks can be easily established but it is important to make these networks living. As there are many different networks in Germany, supporting women in the labour market, good idea would be to combine women in different professions and branches as there are already the ones coming from one branch/profession.

It is recommended that links between urban and rural, or between more developed regions and less developed regions are made.

Women themselves should initiate such networks. Their understanding of local needs and challenges is the key element of the Women@work program. Women themselves do not need to be members of the initiative but will be allowed to benefit from it on ad-hoc basis, nevertheless, efforts on building local networks are to be undertaken.

Conditions of potential transfer of best practices from United Kingdom to Poland

The benefits of the transfer

Participants to the organization and non-members can benefit in variety of ways. First: particular skills are developed via learning programs. Second: gives women more ability express their concerns in their local environments about gender issues. Also, it works as a forum for ideas and opinions exchange, creates broad networking opportunities via meetings, guest speeches and trainings.

Also, it involves women living in the rural areas in the skill development and raises their awareness on gender issues. It strengthens their economic and social presence in communities. This, is particularly relevant in regions with rural areas where women participation in civic and economic life is not sufficient.

Activities to be undertaken to transfer the practice

Existing networks, chambers in different areas could be identified as well as existing circles and networks of women (not necessarily acting in business) should be approached. In Poland, there are still few women networks, and this initiative can use even such a small capacity.

The promotion among women in sparsely populated areas should take place on a very local level (libraries, local shops) and some incentives could be given. The promotion should also be actively made in venues where women entrepreneurs come for administrative purposes.

Minimum requirements for transfer

Selecting organizations and recruiting key people who could combine the existing network resources and attract new organizations and actors. The network should include actors embedded in the rural communities.

Making the initiative not as another one, but a flagship, for example promoted by local government.

The financial support is an important prerequisite for attracting and implementing the practice.

Optimal conditions for the transfer

The learning program should be locally adjusted by individual networks to the needs of women in their communities and the resources of the whole initiatives can be employed to cover the scope and diversity of needs and problems.

An active and up-to-date website portal with events, activities, blog, names and contact details of all the local chapters should be created.

The involvement of different, existing networks and NGOS will add to the promotion and dissemination of the initiative, it will also help to avoid doubling the activities and actions aimed at particular communities.

A strong management and start-up centre with staff recognizing the gender related challenges at a local and global level.

It is helpful involve and attract existing NGOs and local networks in joining in this initiative. Their understanding of local needs and challenges is the key element of the Women@work program. Women themselves do not need to be members of the initiative but will be allowed to benefit from it on ad-hoc basis, nevertheless, efforts on building local networks are to be undertaken.

More attempts from the side of urban areas should be made to create and link with networks of women in rural areas.

Conditions of potential transfer of best practices from United Kingdom to Lithuania

The addressees of the initiative

The addresses are women. It focuses on those women living in rural areas, low paid women, ethnic minority women and young women (less than 30).

Benefits of the practice transfer

Participants to the organization and non-members can benefit in variety of ways. First: particular skills are developed via learning programs. Second: gives women more ability express their concerns in their local environments about gender issues. Also, it works as a forum for ideas and opinions exchange, creates broad networking opportunities via meetings, guest speeches and trainings.

Also, it involves women living in the rural areas in the skill development and raises their awareness on gender issues. It strengthens their economic and social presence in communities. This, is particularly relevant in regions with rural areas where women participation in civic and economic life is not sufficient.

Activities to be undertaken to transfer the practice

Existing networks, chambers in different areas could be identified as well as existing circles and networks of women (not necessarily acting in business) should be approached.

The promotion among women in sparsely populated areas should take place on a very local level (libraries, local shops) and some incentives could be given. The promotion should also be actively made in venues where women entrepreneurs come for administrative purposes.

Minimal requirements for the transfer

Selecting organizations and recruiting key people who could combine the existing network resources and attract new organizations and actors. The network should include actors embedded in the rural communities.

Making the initiative not as another one, but a flagship, for example, promoted by local government.

The financial support is an important prerequisite for attracting and implementing the practice.

Optimal conditions for the transfer

The learning program should be locally adjusted by individual networks to the needs of women in their communities and the resources of the whole initiatives can be employed to cover the scope and diversity of needs and problems.

An active and up-to-date website portal with events, activities, blog, names and contact details of all the local chapters should be created.

The involvement of different, existing networks and NGOS will add to the promotion and dissemination of the initiative, it will also help to avoid doubling the activities and actions aimed at particular communities.

A strong management and start-up centre with staff recognizing the gender related challenges at a local and global level.

The promotion of this initiative can include the dissemination of success stories of women working in executive positions who have been involved in such networks and who contribute to such initiative

It is recommended that some guidelines and materials for training women is available. The organized workshops should be based on real business life situations and be based on broad-minded approach, focusing on leadership elements.

Conditions of potential transfer of best practices from United Kingdom to Latvia

The addressees of the initiative

The addresses are women. It focuses on those women living in rural areas, low paid women, ethnic minority women and young women (less than 30).

Benefits of the practice transfer (for addressees and region)

Participants to the organization and non-members can benefit in variety of ways. First: particular skills are developed via learning programs. Second: gives women more ability express their concerns in their local environments about gender issues. Also, it works as a forum for ideas and opinions exchange, creates broad networking opportunities via meetings, guest speeches and trainings.

Also, it involves women living in the rural areas in the skill development and raises their awareness on gender issues. It strengthens their economic and social presence in communities. This, is particularly relevant in regions with rural areas where women participation in civic and economic life is not sufficient.

Activities to be undertaken to transfer the practice

Existing networks, chambers in different areas could be identified as well as existing circles and networks of women (not necessarily acting in business) should be approached.

The promotion among women in sparsely populated areas should take place on a very local level (libraries, local shops) and some incentives could be given. The promotion should also be actively made in venues where women entrepreneurs come for administrative purposes.

Minimal requirements for the transfer

Selecting organizations and recruiting key people who could combine the existing network resources and attract new organizations and actors. The network should include actors embedded in the rural communities.

Making the initiative not as another one, but a flagship, for example, promoted by local government.

The financial support is an important prerequisite for attracting and implementing the practice.

Optimal conditions for the transfer

The learning program should be locally adjusted by individual networks to the needs of women in their communities and the resources of the whole initiatives can be employed to cover the scope and diversity of needs and problems.

An active and up-to-date website portal with events, activities, blog, names and contact details of all the local chapters should be created.

The involvement of different, existing networks and NGOS will add to the promotion and dissemination of the initiative, it will also help to avoid doubling the activities and actions aimed at particular communities.

A strong management and start-up centre with staff recognizing the gender related challenges at a local and global level.

It is recommended that this initiative serves as an umbrella, united platform mainly for information and consultation purpose.

The inclusion of existing NGOs who can act as starting agents to implement the practice can be helpful.

Their understanding of local needs and challenges by the particular networks with NGOs and other stakeholders is the key element of the Women@work program..

1.6. Ambassadors for Women's entrepreneurship

Conditions of potential transfer of best practices from Sweden to Germany

The addressees of the initiative

The addressees are young women as well as students at educational institutions. The broader audience is the whole society and other successful women entrepreneurs who can be involved in such undertakings.

The benefits of the transfer

The increase in the number of women business start-ups in the region.

Change of mindset in the society in terms of entrepreneurship as a career choice for women (entering labour market or already on the labour market as employees).

Promotion of the selected entrepreneurs and their enterprises in regions via Ambassador tasks.

Skills and experience development among future women entrepreneurs.

The emergence of local, informal networks among women who benefit from the programme.

Activities to be undertaken to transfer the practice

A high prestige as a feature of his practice is necessary. The nomination for woman - the ambassadors should be a great honor for her, involve the strengthening of her social image and should be done in a solemn and momentous atmosphere. Appropriated social campaign preceding the selection of women - the ambassadors would help select the best candidates.

Minimal requirements for the transfer

It is recommended that there is an ongoing selection and recruitment of women ambassadors from different industries and locations. Ambassadors should be dedicated and engaged entrepreneurs, driven by the concern of the women entrepreneurship challenge issue.

Some basic funding for the activity is required like for example for good and sufficient promotion of the initiative in the local media as well as operational activities.

This practice is already existing in many European countries, also in Germany. The purpose would be to strengthen the transfer by further promotion and development of Women Ambassador activities and engage Women from Chambers of Craft networks to participate as ambassadors for promotion of entrepreneurship in craft area too.

Optimal conditions for the transfer

To make the initiative work at its best, there should be interest from educational institutions at all levels secured.

To develop and strengthen the network of participants in their future career on the labour market.

It is important to link the interests of potential women entrepreneurs with their Ambassadors. Also flexible timing in terms mentor availability, shadowing opportunities because the target groups are also women already employed.

Some testimonials from those who already benefited can secure better conditions for further transfer therefore Chambers of Commerce and Chambers of Craft can become members in such initiative to secure the provision of successful and dedicated entrepreneurs.

Conditions of potential transfer of best practices from Sweden to Poland

The addressees of the initiative

The addressees are young women as well as students at educational institutions. The broader audience is the whole society and other successful women entrepreneurs who can be involved in such undertakings.

Benefits of the practice transfer (for addressees and region)

The increase in the number of women business start-ups in the region.

Change of mindset in the society in terms of entrepreneurship as a career choice for women (entering labour market or already on the labour market as employees).

Promotion of the selected entrepreneurs and their enterprises in regions via Ambassador tasks.

Skills and experience development among future women entrepreneurs.

The emergence of local, informal networks among women who benefit from the programme.

Activities to be undertaken to transfer the practice

A high prestige as a feature of his practice is necessary. The nomination for women - the ambassadors should be a great honor for her, involve the strengthening of her social image and should be done in a solemn and momentous atmosphere. Appropriated social campaign preceding the selection of women - the ambassadors would help select the best candidates.

Minimal requirements for the transfer

It is recommended that there is an ongoing selection and recruitment of women ambassadors from different industries and locations. Ambassadors should be dedicated and engaged entrepreneurs, driven by the concern of the women entrepreneurship challenge issue.

Some basic funding for the activity is required like for example for good and sufficient promotion of the initiative in the local media as well as operational activities.

This practice is already existing in many European countries, also in Poland. The purpose would be to strengthen the transfer by further promotion and development of Women Ambassador activities.

Optimal conditions for the transfer

To make the initiative work at its best, there should be interest from educational institutions at all levels secured.

To develop and strengthen the network of participants in their future career on the labour market.

Some testimonials from those who already benefited can secure better conditions for further transfer.

It is important to link the interests of potential women entrepreneurs with their Ambassadors. Also flexible timing in terms mentor availability, shadowing opportunities because the target groups are also women already employed.

Conditions of potential transfer of best practices from Sweden to Lithuania

The addressees of the initiative

The project can be implemented in each country, region and town. Women ambassadors represent different regions of the country, various company sizes, industry sectors, entrepreneurial backgrounds, ages, and experience.

Benefits of the practice transfer (for addressees and region)

The transfer of this practice can make significant contributions to labour market growth. Women's businesses are often found in the services industry such as business services, recreation, hotel and restaurant activities, retail trade and personal services. Women's businesses are thus a strong force in the creation of new job opportunities and are a contributing factor in the transition from a production economy to a services economy.

The implementation of this practice can make significant contributions to economic growth and to poverty reduction. In the United States, for example, women-owned firms are growing at more than double the rate of all other firms. [US Department of Commerce 2010] Nowadays only a country with high business start-up rates (especially women businesses) is not risking economic stagnation.

Women entrepreneurship has a large impact on future generation in each country. More women entrepreneurs on the market, the better the return on investment in the education of girls. Women entrepreneur is able to find a work-life balance that suits them, spend more of their income on the health and education. All this should boost economic growth and labour productivity in the future.

Activities to be undertaken to transfer the practice

A high prestige as a feature of his practice is necessary. The nomination for woman - the ambassadors should be a great honor for her, involve the strengthening of her social image and should be done in a solemn and momentous atmosphere. Appropriated social campaign preceding the selection of women - the ambassadors would help select the best candidates.

Minimal requirements for the transfer

The choice of Women Ambassadors is crucial. The cooperation between the implementing institution and the business sector partner in choosing the women ambassadors is necessary. Candidates must own a successful business, must be recognized as professional with high standards and ethics, demonstrate leadership skills and must accept and commit to active participation in becoming an expert and a mentor to others. The project should receive the Honorary Patronage of the VIP (for example the most popular public women in each country).

Optimal conditions for the transfer

The social government campaign, which will break stereotypes and build an friendly environment for women to create their own opportunities in business would be very supportive for implementation of the practice. In the society the recognition of the fact that maximizing opportunity and advancement for women is a business issue, just as fundamental as productivity, quality, or product development must be increased.

The strong partnerships across organizations (the chamber of commerce and chamber of handicrafts too), working towards the popularization and advertising in job offices, university, schools the idea of women entrepreneurship will strengthen the transfer of this practice.

It would be recommended the creation in the Internet by government the network of Women Ambassadors, who will support open-minded women who have just started and are growing their own business. Members come together to share knowledge, best practices, contacts, and benefit from strategic partnership.

EU or other funding can be desirable to facilitate a start of this project. It would be good also to have the chamber of commerce and chamber of handicrafts as participants in an ambassador choice, as well as Ministries of Economics and the Ministry of Education Youth.

Conditions of potential transfer of best practices from Sweden to Latvia

The addressees of the initiative

The project can be implemented in each country, region and town. Women ambassadors represent different regions of the country, various company sizes, industry sectors, entrepreneurial backgrounds, ages, and experience.

Benefits of the practice transfer (for addressees and region)

The transfer of this practice can make significant contributions to economic growth and to poverty reduction. In the United States, for example, women-owned firms are growing at more than double the rate of all other firms. [US Department of Commerce 2010] Nowadays only a country with high business start-up rates (especially women businesses) is not risking economic stagnation.

Women entrepreneurship has a large impact on future generation in each country. Women generally spend more of their income on health, education and well-being of their families and communities than men do. All this should boost economic growth and labour productivity in the future

Activities to be undertaken to transfer the practice

A high prestige as a feature of his practice is necessary. The nomination for woman - the ambasadors should be a great honor for her, involve the strengthening of her social image and should be done in a solemn and momentous atmosphere. Appropriated social campaign preceding the selection of women - the ambassadors would help select the best candidates.

Minimal requirements for the transfer

This initiative requires recruitment of participants who can afford payment for the training and coaching programme. Appropriate fee needs to be set so that it was not too high.

Participant groups need to be well-defined beforehand (existing entrepreneurs or existing plus future entrepreneurs)

The choice of Women Ambassadors is crucial. The cooperation between the implementing institution and the business sector partner in choosing the women ambassadors is necessary. Candidates must own a successful business, must be recognized as professional with high standards and ethics, demonstrate leadership skills and must accept and commit to active participation in becoming an expert and a mentor to others. The project should receive the Honorary Patronage of the VIP (for example the most popular public women in each country).

Optimal conditions for the transfer

EU or other funding can be desirable to facilitate a start of this project. It would be good also to have the chamber of commerce and chamber of handicrafts as participants in an ambassador choice, as well as Ministries of Economics and the Ministry of Education Youth.

The government, local community can do a lot to facility the implementation of this practice. Societal attitudes and social beliefs discourage some women from even considering starting a business. So the awareness campaign, which will break stereotypes and build an friendly environment for these skilled women to create their own opportunities would be very supportive for the practice.

The government can also establish "The Women Ambassador Office". This creation will reflect each government's policy to promote gender equality and it will be a good promotion tool for the practice. Using information and communication technologies the official women network portal can be created to share women's experiences. In this portal knowledge of women's entrepreneurship and of the industries in which many women entrepreneurs are active should be disseminated. Facts, statistics and knowledge will be compiled in order to highlight and disseminate knowledge about women's entrepreneurship in different areas to different target groups.

Advertising this program in job offices, universities, schools especially in March, when international Women's day is celebrated, would be highly recommended.

2. The transfer of the best practices, which improve the elderly participation on the BSR labour market

2.1. Senior policy in working life

Conditions of potential transfer of best practices from Norway to Germany

The necessity of implementation

Hanseatic Parliament, Schwerin Chamber of Skilled Crafts and Hamburg Institute of International Economics participated in the evaluation of this practice's implementation conditions.

As the Eurostat data show, economic activity of German people aged 55 to 64 is above the European average. However, a rising trend could be observed from 2004. It was confirmed by the three German Partners that low economic activity of seniors is regarded as a problem. This is the argument for taking this practice into account.

Legal conditions of the implementation

No regulation barriers which could potentially disturb the practice's implementation process were noticed. This practice is not contradictory to national or local policies and with the traditional way of thinking or acting. Moreover, Partners said that German institutions are interested in implementing this kind of practice and they are experienced and skilled enough.

Organizational conditions of the implementation

The proposed practice requires the cooperation between organizations of the labour market, local or national agencies and enterprise federations in strategy formulation and establishment of partnerships. The implementation of proposed solution allows for creation of a senior-friendly environment – promoting the inclusion of the senior citizens into labour market.

The main problem is to encourage the beneficiaries to display enough initiative and motivation to participate in it. Two of the Partners agreed that the implementation of this practice requires full engagement and collaboration of different bodies and organizations across the country.

Financial conditions of the implementation

There are is common opinion among the Partners in relation to the access to the external sources of financing this kind of solutions. In the opinion of the two Partners, the necessity of submitting complex, formal applications for external funding could discourage potentially interested bodies from starting the activity.

Is it possible to implement the initiative in Germany? – needed support, threats and benefits

Germany is implementing a few initiatives similar to the proposed one (pointed out by HWWI) — for example, the German Federal Ministry of Employment and Social Affairs co-finances programmes of the European Union (European Social Fund) to foster employment of the elderly by helping employers to create an appropriate workplace situation that accounts for the needs of seniors.

Moreover, German Federal Ministries aim at strengthening the public awareness of the potentials and resources of the elderly by public promotion measures which directly point to the positive social and economic effects of a better integration of the seniors.

In the estimation of the risk of this initiative's failure, the Partners were not unanimous:

— one claimed that the risk is rather high,
— the other one contended that the risk is not so high, whereas the last one did not have any option.

This initiative has to be conducted on the macro level (local or national authorities, organizations and employers or market bodies).

As one of the Partners underlined, addressing the practice to persons who are subject to the risk and take the efforts related to the re-entering the labour market has to rely on the age-appropriate activities. Disability-sensitive working facilities hold out the prospect for this. Therefore, it is considered as being very important to train supervisors who accompany those persons as part of a regained or gained workforce in managing their workaday belongings at the workplace.

Conditions of potential transfer of best practices from Norway to Poland

The necessity of implementation

The possibilities and conditions of initiative implementation in Poland were evaluated by two project's partners:

— PP10 Gdańsk University of Technology
— PP13 BFPT Bialystok Foundation of Professional Training

In Poland, the employment rate of senior citizens is the lowest among the BSR countries. Low economic activity of this part of population is one of the most serious problems of the Polish labour market. According to that, many initiatives were taken to improve the employability of the elderly. Most of these programmes were addressed directly to them and aimed to encourage seniors to prolong their professional activity. Nevertheless, initiatives like the ones presented here were not noticed.

Legal conditions of the implementation

The partners presented extremely different opinions on the question whether the current regulations allow for the implementation of the proposed practice or not. However, they agreed that existing Polish regulations are not flexible enough and could hinder taking particular actions and solutions which are crucial in this initiative. Moreover, implementing this practice would probably require obtaining additional permission.

Organizational conditions of the implementation

Both Partners agreed that implementation requires full engagement and collaboration of different bodies and organizations across the country. Partners presented extremely different opinions on the issue of the correspondence of this practice with local/ national strategic documents and competence of local authorities/ institutions/ other potential partners. However, Partners agreed that local authorities/ institutions/

partners cannot offer the necessary support for implementation this practice in interested organizations.

Financial conditions of the implementation

In Poland there are no or very little own sources among institutions potentially interested in implementing the practice and access to external (public/private) sources for financing this kind of project is limited. The implementation will probably require applying for EU funding which is not guaranteed.

Is it possible to implement the initiative in Poland? – needed support, threats and benefits

The risk of failure of implementation of this practice was estimated as high.

The implementation requires establishing a cooperation platform – in Poland potential beneficiaries of such practice would not display sufficient motivation to participate in this practice /there are not enough incentives for participating in this practice. Moreover, this practice, in the Partner's opinion, could be contradictory to the traditional way of thinking and acting in our country/region in terms of integration of economically excluded groups into the labour market.

Support, i.e. strategic consulting, is needed at the government level. Many NGOs already work in similar fields. It is worth to cooperate to work out a particular result.

Conditions of potential transfer of best practices from Norway to Lithuania

The necessity of implementation

The only Partner from Lithuania which participated in the evaluation of the possibility of the best practice transfer was PP5 VPU, the Lithuanian University of Educational Sciences.

In Lithuania the low economic activity of the elderly has been regarded as a problem. Although the employment rate among the seniors is above EU average, it is still not satisfactory. According to the Eurostat data, in 2010 only 48.6% of seniors (people aged 55–64) were still working.

The process of the inclusion of the seniors into labour market in Lithuania is at the initial phase. Using the experiences from Norway could accelerate the preparation of the senior policy.

Legal conditions of the implementation

There are not any legal barriers in Lithuania for implementation of the initiative, because its aim and guidelines are compatible with national/local policies and strategic documents.

Organizational conditions of the implementation

In the Partners opinion, there are not many organizational barriers to implementing the proposed practice.

Although the proposed practice implementation could require a complex formal application for external funding, local government/institutions/partners can offer necessary support, as they have sufficient experience, skills and competences necessary for implementing this kind of practice. Moreover, this practice is not contradictory to traditional way of thinking and acting in Lithuania in terms of integration of economically excluded groups into the labour market

Financial conditions of the implementation

According to the fact that in the Partner's opinion implementation of this practice could require applying for EU funding which is not guaranteed and organizations/ institutions do not possess enough founds for financing the whole implementation process, potential barriers could arise.

Is it possible to implement the initiative in Lithuania? – needed support, threats and benefits

The risk of failure was estimated as rather low.

One of the Partners suggested implementing the initiative at the government level in order to encourage the entrepreneurs to employ the seniors e.g. by tax policy (reducing social taxes).

It is necessary to introduce some regulations allowing for the practice implementation.

At the beginning, the initiative has to be conducted on the government/ local level. It requires engagement and collaboration of different bodies and organizations across the whole country.

Promotion activities helping to improve the awareness of the ageing population problems are definitely needed.

Conditions of potential transfer of best practices from Norway to Latvia

The necessity of implementation

Partner 6, VISC State Education Centre, was helpful in evaluating the possibility of this practice implementation. There are no similar projects in Latvia. There is an on-going debate in Latvia about seniors in the labour market. 70% of enterprises employ seniors but only 7% of enterprises think of improving the work environment for them. The Ministry of Welfare supported the EU initiative in 2012 "Senior friendly enterprise" (5 enterprises were chosen as the most senior friendly ones).

Legal conditions of the implementation

In the Partner's opinion, this practice does not require additional permissions by institutions implementing it. Moreover, the aim and guidelines of the proposed initiative are not contrary to national/local policies and strategic documents.

Organizational conditions of the implementation

The limitations of implementation of the proposed practice are result rather from the lack of awareness and willingness to action than from the real organizational barriers. As the Partner said, in Latvia local government/institutions/partners have sufficient experience, skills and competences necessary for implementing this kind of practice.

Financial conditions of the implementation

A few potential financial barriers have arisen, because in Latvia institutions which may interested in implementing this kind of solution do not possess the sufficient funds. In addition, there is a limited access to information about potential external financial sources for this kind of project and limited access to external (public/private) sources for financing.

Is it possible to implement the initiative in Latvia? – needed support, threats and benefits

The main threat is that there is no interest among local government/institutions/partners in implementing this kind of practice.

The proposed activities include the provision of a better and more inclusive working environment for all workers, as well as the facilitation of cooperation among labour, employer and government organizations and authorities concerning senior policy.

The implementation of this practice in Latvia requires engagement and collaboration of different bodies and organizations across the whole country.

As potential beneficiaries of such practice would not display sufficient motivation to participate in this practice, promotional activities aimed at helping to improve the awareness of benefits from employing seniors are needed.

2.2. Senior enterprices – experience never ages

Conditions of potential transfer of best practices from Ireland to Germany

The necessity of implementation

Partners participating in the diagnose of possibilities and conditions of initiative's implementation were as follow:

— PP1 – Hanseatic Parliament
— PP2 – Schwerin Chamber of Skilled Crafts
— PP3 – HWWI Hamburg Institute of International Economics

Low economic activity of elderly is regarded as a problem in Germany. All three partners agreed with that (two definitely, one rather). That can be treated as one of the main arguments for initiative's implementation.

The actual demographic structure of German population and it's prognoses for next two decades are very adverse. According to the forecasts of United Nations, in the year 2030 over 49% of German population will be persons aged 50 years old and more. At the same time, economic activity of this group is still lower than in Scandinavian countries: according to Eurostat data in 2011 employment rate in group aged 55–64 in Germany was 59,9% comparing with 72,3% in Sweden.

Legal conditions of the implementation

There are no regulations' barriers that could hinder to implement the initiative. All partners definitely disagreed with the sentence: "In our country/region there are no regulations that allow for implementation of this initiative". In respondents' opinion the law in Germany is flexible enough to take into account actions and solutions proposed in the initiative.

Quite important for success of initiative's implementation is the partner's diagnose that the initiative is compatible with the national and regional policies (and so strategic documents).

Organizational conditions of the implementation

In partners' opinion, local government and different types of institutions should be interested in initiative's implementation. A kind of problem could be with the sufficient experience, skills and competences necessary for efficient implementation. There are not enough institutions that could support the bodies implementing that initiative. Partners emphasized many times that initiative's implementation requires full engagement and collaboration of different bodies and organizations across the whole country or region.

Financial conditions of the implementation

Among significant barriers for initiative's implementation are the financial conditions. In partners' opinion implementation would require applying for EU funding and there are many organizations that do not show the interest in preparation formal applications for this type of external funding. Unfortunately, in Germany this type of funding is very difficult to achieve.

Is it possible to implement the initiative in Germany? – short summary

The risk of failure for this initiative is not very high

There are no legal limitations that might prevent to implement the initiative

There must be build up the coalition of different types of organizations wishing to undertake that challenge

There should be organized workshops, study visits, lectures, presentations – different types of activities that would help to build up the awareness, knowledge and skills needed in realizing that type of initiative

Organization that will decide to implement the initiative needs the support. It would be the best to cooperate with those who already realize that projects (even from abroad). The mentoring and advising in needed

There must be financial support available, including EU funds.

Conditions of potential transfer of best practices from Ireland to Poland

The necessity of implementation

The possibilities and conditions of initiative implementation in Poland were evaluated by two project's partners:

— PP10 Gdańsk University of Technology
— PP13 BFPT Bialystok Foundation of Professional Training

Forecasts of Polish population age structure is very unfavorable. According to data from United Nations, in the year 2030 over 42% of total population will be persons aged 50 years old and more. At the same, employment rate for Poles aged 50+ is one of the lowest in Europe. According to Eurostat data in population aged 55-64 years old in 2011 it was 45,3% among men and only 25,2% among the women.

Low economic activity among the elderly is recognized as one of significant economic problems in Poland, and in partners' opinion implementation of proposed initiative would help to solve it. "In Poland there are innovative projects under the European Social Fund, which addresses issues relating to the activity of people in the age 50+, for example *Innovation 50 + program testing and implementation of new methods of maintenance activity of employees over 50 years old* implemented by Bialystok School of Economics and partners (www.pracujemy50plus.pl)"6, "there are also projects which offer similar involvement of elderly but they are not so complex, e.g. the project *Mature entreopreneurship* realised by Vivodaship Labor Office"7. Nevertheless, both of the partners agreed that this type of the initiative is needed in Poland..

Legal conditions of the implementation

There are no regulations' barriers that could hinder to implement the initiative. Both of the partners rather disagreed with the sentence: "In our country/region there are no regulations that allow for implementation of this initiative". In respondent's opinion the law in Poland is flexible enough to take into account actions and solutions proposed in the initiative.

In partners opinion, issues related to elderly economic activation are not pointedly enough put into a national/regional policy and strategic documents. Crisis and high unemployment among youngers decide, that implementation of another initiative addressed to elderly could be difficult.

Organizational conditions of the implementation

In partners opinion, there should be the interest in the initiative's implementation among different types of organizations, including local government. There can be the problem with not sufficient motivation among beneficiaries to participate in the initiative. That opinion comes to the partners after realization in their regions several initiatives addressed to persons aged 50+.

Organizations responsible for implementation should have enough sufficient skills and experience in implementation, but they could not account on any special support from other bodies operating in the region. The only way to realize that type of initia-

---

[6] Quote of the answer received in the evaluation process
[7] Quote of the answer received in the evaluation process

tive efficient would be to build up interdisciplinary (different types of organizations) team (consortium) involved in.

Financial conditions of the implementation

The initiative's implementation can be limited or impossible because of lack of funds. In partners opinion there is no enough private and public funds that could be directed for realizing this type of initiative. There would be a need to apply for EU funds and organization which decides for implementation will have to prepare the complex, formal application for external funding.

Is it possible to implement the initiative in Poland? – short summary

The risk of failure for this initiative was evaluated as low

There are no legal limitations that might prevent to implement the initiative

The issues of elderly and their economic activity should be put into the regional policy documents as priorities

There is still very adverse image of elderly among the Polish society, it must be changed. The promotion activities/projects are needed

There must be promoted facts/ examples showing the economic/professional potential of the elderly

There must be build up the coalition of different types of organizations wishing to undertake that challenge.

Organization that will decide to implement the initiative needs the support. It would be the best to cooperate with those who already realize that projects (even from abroad). The mentoring and advising in needed

There must be financial support available, including EU funds

Conditions of potential transfer of best practices from Ireland to Lithuania

The necessity of implementation

There was only one partner from Lithuania participating in the diagnose of possibilities and conditions of initiative's implementation:

— PP5 – VPU Lithuanian University of Educational Sciences

The actual demographic structure of Lithuanian population and it's prognoses for next two decades are similar to other eastern EU member states: the population is shrinking and society is going to aging. According to the forecasts of United Nations, in the year 2030 total population of Lithuania will be fewer of number over 25% comparing to the statistics from the year 1990, and over 39% of Lithuanian will be persons aged 50 years old and more.

In partners' opinion, initiatives similar to this presented above are still not present in Lithuania.

Legal conditions of the implementation

There are no regulations' barriers that could hinder to implement the initiative. Partner who did evaluate the conditions of implementation rather disagree with the sentence: "In our country/region there are regulations that allow for implementation of this initiative". In partner's opinion the law in Lithuania is flexible enough to take into account actions and solutions proposed in the initiative.

Quite important for success of initiative's implementation is the partner's diagnose that the initiative is compatible with the national and regional policies (and so strategic documents).

Organizational conditions of the implementation

In partners' opinion, local government and different types of institutions should be interested in initiative's implementation. There are organizations that have enough experience to take the responsibility for implementation. "In Lithuania there already has been a public company "Versli Lietuva" which helps people to start their own business. It does not matter that you are 18 or 50 years old you can ask them and they will prepare the business starting packets, which includes trainings and mentoring, also there are funds for business start". It can be expected that government (regional/local authorities) will be able to offer needed support for other bodies that would implement the initiative. Partner emphasized that initiative's implementation requires full engagement and collaboration of different bodies and organizations across the whole country or region.

Financial conditions of the implementation

Among significant barriers for initiative's implementation are the financial conditions. There are no public or private funds that could be addressed for realizing that type of initiative. In partner's opinion implementation would require applying for EU funding (answer definitely agree) and there are many organizations that do not show the interest in preparation formal applications for this type of external funding. In partner's opinion there is also a problem with access to information about potential external financial sources.

Is it possible to implement the initiative in Lithuania? – short summary

The risk of failure for this initiative is not very high

There are no legal limitations that might prevent to implement the initiative

There must be build up the coalition of different types of organizations wishing to undertake that challenge

Partner's proposition was "to organize the country level conference for elder people and to show them that the age to run a business is not a problem; to invite for this conference people who started their business near the age of 50 and present their success stories to elder people in Lithuania"

Crucial condition for initiative's implementation in Lithuania is the financial support from EU funds. Because there are problems with getting the information about available external sources of finances, the new tools and methods of that information distributions should be developed and implemented.

Conditions of potential transfer of best practices from Ireland to Latvia

The necessity of implementation

There was only one project's partner who participated in the process of implementation's evaluation. That was PP6 VISC State Education Centre.

Age structure of Latvian population is not so bad nowadays and in the future. According to the forecasts of United Nations, in the year 2030 over 40,5% of Latvian population will be persons aged 50 years old and more. 26% of the total population will be persons younger than 25 years old. Alarming phenomenon is the process of population's shrinking. In the year 2030 the Latvian population will be probably 30% smaller than in the year 1990.

As it was noted in the evaluation, the aging processes and low economic activity of older persons are not regarded in Latvian society as real problem.

In the country and region there are not implemented similar practices as this one. Nevertheless there have been already realized some other projects addressed to older persons to convince them to higher economic activity. "ESF co-financed program support for starting self-employment or entrepreneurship from January 2010 in Latvia was implemented. The program offered consultations, training, and financing for those who wanted to start their own business and recently founded businesses. The program was available in all regions of Latvia. Training included: basics of entrepreneurship, legal framework of entrepreneurship, financial management, accounting and taxes, marketing basics, etc. During the program lifecycle 1624 persons from different age groups were trained. There are some other project based initiatives related to the Senior enterprises – experience never ages, e.g., EU BSR Project Best Agers"[8].

Legal conditions of the implementation

There are no regulations' barriers that could hinder to implement the initiative. The partner rather disagreed with the sentence: "In our country/region there are no regulations that allow for implementation of this initiative". In respondent's opinion the

---

[8] Quote of the answer received in the evaluation process

law in Latvia is flexible enough to take into account actions and solutions proposed in the initiative.

Quite important for success in initiative's implementation is its compatibility with the national and regional policies (and so strategic documents).

Organizational conditions of the implementation

In partner's opinion, local government should be interested in initiative's implementation. Not sufficient motivation among beneficiaries to participate in the initiative and not enough incentives for participating in the practice, those are significant barriers in the initiative's implementation.

Different types of institutions involved so far in elderly activation do have some experience, skills and competences needed to implement the practice, but they rather could not account on any support in their activities from national or regional authorities.

Financial conditions of the implementation

The funds for initiative's implementation are main problems. In partner's opinion there is no enough private and public funds that could be directed for realizing this type of initiative. There would be a need to apply for EU funds and organization which decides for implementation will have to prepare the complex, formal application for external funding.

Is it possible to implement the initiative in Latvia? – short summary

The risk of failure for this initiative was evaluated as high

There are no legal limitations that might prevent to implement the initiative

There must be build up the coalition of different types of organizations wishing to undertake that challenge

Organization that will decide to implement the initiative needs the support. It would be the best to cooperate with those who already realize that projects (even from abroad). The mentoring and advising in needed

There must be financial support available, including EU funds

Because of low interest among beneficiaries, the substantive and organizational support is needed (for those persons 50+ who decide to start their own business including assistance in finding partners: training, financial assistance, a database of potential business partners)

Different forms of cooperation with persons 50+ should be developed: entrepreneurs, professionals in various fields of business, interested in providing advisory services (mentoring) for new entrepreneurs, including those aged 50 + (group and individual meetings with counsellors)

There is a great need of rising the awareness among the society that aging processes are harmful for the economy and professional activity of persons aged 50+ is one of the ways to mitigate the crisis in the future.

2.3. Flexible work practices

Conditions of potential transfer of best practices from Sweden to Germany

The necessity of implementation

Partners participating in the diagnose of possibilities and conditions of initiative's implementation were as follow:

— PP1 – Hanseatic Parliament
— PP2 – Schwerin Chamber of Skilled Crafts
— PP3 – HWWI Hamburg Institute of International Economics

All three partners agreed, that in Germany there is a problem with low economic activity of persons aged 55+ and different initiatives in that field should be implemented. They also agreed that in Germany there haven't been already realized initiatives as that one. One of the partners written in the evaluation form "We are not aware of distinct firms which pursue the aims mentioned here in this complexity, but in general, the topic of ageing staff and the necessity of ageing-suitable working conditions gains more importance these days in Germany"9. Summing this up, there is a need and possibility to implement proposed one..

Legal conditions of the implementation

There are no regulations' barriers that could hinder to implement the initiative. All partners disagreed with the sentence: "In our country/region there are no regulations that allow for implementation of this initiative". In respondents' opinion the law in Germany is flexible enough to take into account actions and solutions proposed in the initiative. Nevertheless, that was noted by the partners, that undertaking this practice requires additional permissions by institutions implementing it. As it was put into the original practice's description10, one of the partners who had to agree on initiative's implementation were labor unions.

There is no coincidence between the initiative aims and the aims and guidelines of national and regional policy.

Organizational conditions of the implementation

Organizations who decide to implement the initiative could expect positive reaction from the beneficiaries side (it can be expected that they will be motivated enough to participate in the initiative) and support from the local government and professional institutions operating in the region. In partners opinion they do have sufficient skills and experience necessary for implementing that type of practice.

Financial conditions of the implementation

There is limited access to external sources (in meaning private or public) for financing this type of initiatives in Germany, so there would be a need to apply for EU funding, which is not guaranteed. Fortunately, there shouldn't be any technical problem with preparing the proper application, because there is a lot of information about potential

---

9 Quote of the answer received in the evaluation process
10 http://www.eurofound.europa.eu/areas/populationandsociety/cases/se004.htm

EU financial sources and practical support in writing the application. There is only the question, if German organizations are interested in the initiative and applying for EU funds. Partners who participated in the evaluation did not have one point of view. The answers for the question: "In our country/region there is no interest among different institutions in implementing this kind of practice" were as follow:

— rather agree
— I have no opinion
— rather disagree.

Is it possible to implement the initiative in Germany? – short summary

The risk of failure for this initiative was evaluated as not very high.

The initiative has to be conducted on the firm level. Compared to the businesses themselves, governmental authorities suffer a lack of information of how to best motivate employees of younger and older age to adopt the guidelines of an ageing enterprise. Likewise, actors on the firm level are more capable to consider and evaluate risks and chances of such an initiative.

There are no legal limitations that might prevent to implement the initiative on national level, but some additional permissions can be needed, e.g. labor unions opinion.

There must be build up the coalition of different types of organizations wishing to undertake that challenge.

There can be expected the support for the firms implementing the initiative, but the most important is to find their own way to handle those issues.

There should be build up the awareness and knowledge among the entrepreneurs about that kind of solutions, they do not know about them and are not interest in implementation.

There must be financial support available, including EU funds.

Conditions of potential transfer of best practices from Sweden to Poland

The necessity of implementation

The possibilities and conditions of initiative implementation in Poland were evaluated by two project's partners:

— PP1 – Hanseatic Parliament
— PP2 – Schwerin Chamber of Skilled Crafts
— PP3 – HWWI Hamburg Institute of International Economics

Low economic activity of older persons is one of the main problems on labour market in Poland. There have been realized several programmes/project/activities lead by different types of institutions to change that situation. Most of them have been addressed directly to older persons and there aim was to encourage this group to prolong their professional activity. There is still not enough activities directed to the entrepreneurs to show them the potential of older workers and convince them to implement different tools and methods of age management in their companies. The age management is the concept that Polish entrepreneurs and managers do not know well enough, and are not interested in its implementation.

There have been not implemented yet similar initiatives, as presented. "There are not such complex projects, but there are several which try to promote individual actions e.g training for managers in the issues of age management"11. In partners opinion it's very good idea and should be promoted in Poland.

Legal conditions of the implementation

There are no regulations' barriers that could hinder to implement the initiative. Both of the partners rather disagreed with the sentence: "In our country/region there are no regulations that allow for implementation of this initiative". In respondent's opinion the law in Poland is flexible enough to take into account actions and solutions proposed in the initiative. In last year there have been settle new regulations in Poland, related to the flexicurity on the labour market.

---

[11] Quote of the answer received in the evaluation process

The idea of flexible work is compatible with the national/regional policy and strategic documents.

Organizational conditions of the implementation

It can be difficult to implement this initiative because of organizations' lack of experience. Both of the partners agreed with the sentence: "In our country/region local government/institutions/partners do not have sufficient experience, skills and competences necessary for implementing this kind of practice". There is not available support for organizations interested in implementation. Partners agreed with the sentence: "In our country/region local government/institutions/partners cannot offer necessary support for other bodies that would implement this practice". It would be also difficult to find entrepreneurs, employers and employees interested in the activities included in the initiative. Both partners again agreed with the sentence: "In our country/region potential beneficiaries of such practice would not display sufficient motivation to participate in this practice /there are not enough incentives for participating in this practice".

Even if the risk of failure for this practice was evaluates as low, it can be said that in Poland implementation can be very difficult.

Financial conditions of the implementation

The initiative's implementation can be limited or impossible because of lack of funds. Both of the partners rather agreed with two sentences: "In our country/region there are no or very little own sources among institutions potentially interested in implementing this kind of solution" and "In our country/region there is a limited access to external (public/private) sources for financing this kind of project".

The only possibility to get funds is applying for EU funds. It can be the reason that would discourage organizations potentially interested in implementation.

Is it possible to implement the initiative in Poland? – short summary

The risk of failure for this initiative was evaluated as low, nevertheless there are several arguments that makes this initiative difficult to implement in Poland

There is a great need to build the awareness about the ageing process among managers; potential of older workers, methods and tools of age management.

There is a great need to build the awareness of flexible work conditions benefits.

There are no legal limitations that might prevent to implement the initiative.

There should be develop the knowledge in the field of how to use the flexible work methods.

There is a need of training, coaching, analysis of case studies in that issue.

Local governments and other institutions should prepare an offer of support for the institutions interested in flexible work conditions implementation.

There must be financial support available, including EU funds.

Conditions of potential transfer of best practices from Sweden to Lithuania

The necessity of implementation

There was only one partner participating in the diagnose of possibilities and conditions of initiative's implementation:

— PP5 – VPU Lithuanian University of Educational Sciences

Partner agreed, that in Lithuania there is a problem with low economic activity of persons aged 55+ and different initiatives in that field should be implemented. He also agreed that in Lithuania there haven't been already realized initiatives as that one.

Legal conditions of the implementation

There are no regulations' barriers that could hinder to implement the initiative. Partners rather disagreed with the sentence: "In our country/region there are no regulations that allow for implementation of this initiative". In respondent's opinion the law in Lithuania is flexible enough to take into account actions and solutions proposed in the initiative. It was also noted by the partner, that undertaking this practice would not require any additional permissions by institutions implementing it.

There is no coincidence between the initiative aims and the aims and guidelines of national and regional policy.

Organizational conditions of the implementation

Organizations who decide to implement the initiative could expect positive reaction from the beneficiaries side (it can be expected that they will be motivated enough to participate in the initiative) and support from the local government and professional institutions operating in the region. In partners opinion they do have sufficient skills and experience necessary for implementing that type of practice.

Financial conditions of the implementation

There is limited access to external sources (in meaning private or public) for financing this type of initiatives in Lithuania. The only possibility for initiative's implementation is to get the EU funds, which is not guaranteed. Unfortunately, there can be some technical problems with preparing the proper application, because there is not much information about potential EU financial sources and practical support in writing the application. The problem is also small interest among Lithuanian organizations in the initiative and applying for EU funds.

Is it possible to implement the initiative in Lithuania? – short summary

The risk of failure for this initiative was evaluated as not very high.

There are no legal limitations that might prevent to implement the initiative on national level.

There must be build up the coalition of different types of organizations wishing to undertake that challenge.

There should be build up the awareness and knowledge among the entrepreneurs about that kind of solutions, they do not know about them and are not interest in implementation.

There must be EU financial support available, otherwise it won't be possible to implement the initiative.

There is a great need to build up the information system – there is not enough information about available EU funds for enterprises development.

Conditions of potential transfer of best practices from Sweden to Latvia

The necessity of implementation

There was only one project's partner who participated in the process of implementation's evaluation. That was PP6 VISC State Education Centre.

In partner's opinion low economic activity of older persons needs to be changed, that's why there should be realized different actions to reduce its negative effects.

In Latvia there have been already implement initiatives as proposed above. "There are several initiatives referring to some part of Flexible work practices initiative. Initiative Connect Latvia is implemented by Lattelecom. The aim of this initiative is to train ICT skills to seniors 50+ to promote social inclusion. Since 2011 about 10 000 seniors have been trained in ICT skills in all the regions of Latvia. Till the 100th anniversary of Latvia in 2018 Lattelecom plans to train 30 000 seniors. Similar activity is implemented by National Centre for Education in the project Grandchildren and Grandparents where pupils teach ITC skills to seniors (2011-2013). There is also the initiative Change opportunities for schools. Schools together with local community members look for new, creative and effective ways of taking advantages of the existing resources to change and enliven schools so that they can become a meeting and activity place for all local community members including seniors"[12].

Legal conditions of the implementation

There are no regulations' barriers that could hinder to implement the initiative. The partner rather disagreed with the sentence: "In our country/region there are no regulations that allow for implementation of this initiative". Nonetheless, it was noted that existing regulations are not flexible and implementation would be very difficult.

---

[12] Quote of the answer received in the evaluation process

Quite important for success in initiative's implementation is its compatibility with the national and regional policies (and so strategic documents).

Organizational conditions of the implementation

There should not appear any organizational problems with implementation. Latvian institutions have an experience and skills from previous initiatives similar to this practice:

— learning centres – the council has set up local learning centres that use modern techniques and where workers can pursue formal education or other training, flexibly and at their own pace
— validation – the council validates experience-based knowledge so that workers can more easily move between job categories or employers
— using pensioners as substitutes – employees at two of the council's facilities can continue to work as substitutes after retirement when they reach 64 years old.

It's possible to get the support for the organization that will implement the initiative. There could be also expected the interest in the initiative among employees as its beneficiaries.

Financial conditions of the implementation

It should be possible to find the financial sources for that type of initiative. Nevertheless the most possible source pointed by the respondent were EU funds. If there is a need of extra funds for implementation, interested organization should apply for EU financial support.

Is it possible to implement the initiative in Latvia? – short summary

The risk of failure for this initiative was evaluated as low.

There are no legal limitations that might prevent to implement the initiative, but the law is not flexible so there could be some difficulties.

That is typically enterprise' level initiative, so there is no need to build up the coalition of different types of organizations wishing to undertake that challenge.

There are companies/institutions that has already implement similar solutions (may be not so complex), their knowledge and experience should be presented and shared with those who are planning to implement that initiative.

There must be financial support available, including EU funds.

There is a great need of rising the awareness among the employers about the un-tapped potential of workers aged 55+.

2.4. Higher Vocational Education

Conditions of potential transfer of best practices from Sweden to Germany

The necessity of implementation

Hanseatic Parliament, Schwerin Chamber of Skilled Crafts and Hamburg Institute of International Economics participated in the evaluation of this practice's implementation conditions.

CEDEFOP [http://www.cedefop.europa.eu/EN/Index.aspx] data shows that in Germany:

— the percentage of adults engaged in lifelong learning (7,7%) was in 2009 slightly lower than EU average (9,1%)
— the percentage of seniors, the unemployed and people with relatively low qualifications participating in lifelong learning were all lower than the EU average in 2009.

Partners listed a few initiatives/ solutions similar to the proposed one. For example, similar projects which apply to local labour market requirements and which are managed by local stakeholders like chambers of commerce, chambers of craft etc. have not yet come to our knowledge in the case of Germany. Instead, there are plenty of courses provided by private adult training institutions which focus on general entrepreneurial and management skills, suiting the needs of the labour market demand within special occupational fields and sectors but without particular regard to local markets. On the other hand, chambers of commerce and chambers of craft address the attainment of primary occupational skills by young people rather than adult training tasks. In addition, the German Agency for Labour (Agentur für Arbeit) is facilitating numerous trainings like this, directly targeted at employees that are older than 35+, 47+47+, 50+ and 55+ (see: http://kursnet-finden.arbeitsagentur.de/kurs/kursDetail.do?seite=1&uf=1&bz=%C3%A4ltere&anzahlGesamt=26&anzahlProSeite=200&doNext=detail&anzahlSeite=200&gv=C+091-05&ss=C&ae=74&gpBy=gbZiel&out=gbZiel). Most of these trainings are offered by private institutions — the interested individuals can apply for funding from the agency to pay for this training ("Bildungsgutschein").

On the other hand, Partners stated that no solutions like the proposed one exist in Germany, so it could be worth to adapt and implement the practice.

Legal conditions of the implementation

There are no organizational barriers for implementing the practices like the proposed one. The educational system in Germany is quite developed and tries to meet the market needs. The proposed initiative is not contradictory to national/local policies.

Organizational conditions of the implementation

The existing German regulations are flexible enough and they should allow to take into account particular actions and solutions that are crucial element of proposed practice. Although the Partners did not agree as to the evaluation of the experience, competence, skills and interest of local authorities/ institution in the implementation of the initiative, they did not doubt that these organizations can offer necessary support. The considered solution is complementary to traditional way of thinking and acting in Germany in terms of integration of the economically excluded groups into the labour market.

Financial conditions of the implementation

The Partners' opinions concerning the possibilities of financing the practice implementation from own or external founds are divided. One of them feared that the necessity of making a complex formal application for external funding of such an initiative discourages potentially interested bodies/organizations/businesses from doing so. The other one suggested that implementation of this practice could require applying for EU funding which is not guaranteed.

Is it possible to implement the initiative in Germany? – needed support, threats and benefits

The risk of failure of proposed practice implementation was estimated as low.

Activities suggested by project Partners are conductive to successful completion. First of all, chambers and other institutions which represent the interest of local firms would have to acknowledge the economic advantages of adult training with a focus on local needs. This insight is indispensible for the second step of collaboration. Local authorities are eventually helpful in providing access to information that addresses overall economic and demographic developments on a macro level, but the aid of authorities should be claimed by firms and their representatives since otherwise governmental need will not be accepted.

Some support is needed. For example, market institutions have to initiate and organize such a process by themselves. Also access to financial support by local authorities could stimulate the private engagement. However, each funding scheme has to be sensitive to the free-rider problem as a general problem of subsidizing private initiatives.

Conditions of potential transfer of best practices from Sweden to Poland

The necessity of implementation

The surveys and statistics show that Poland – in comparison to other European countries – has one of the lowest rates of adult participation in continuous learning. (see: **Introduction**)

CEDEFOP [http://www.cedefop.europa.eu/EN/Index.aspx] data shows that in Poland:

— fewer adults are involved in lifelong learning as compared to EU as a whole (5.3% and 9.1% respectively),

— although the participation levels of older and lower-educated adults are greater in Poland than in the EU in general, the rate of individuals participating in LLP slightly decreased between 2010 and 2011.

The Gdansk University of Technology and the Bialystok Foundation of Professional Training evaluated the possibility of implementation of Swedish practice of vocational education.

They stated that in Poland there are no solutions similar to the proposed one, so its implementation could help to solve some problems, e.g. the mismatch between skills and labour market needs.

Legal conditions of the implementation

Partners agreed that in Poland there are regulations that allow for the implementation of proposed solution, however one of the Partners noticed that these regulations could be not flexible enough to allow for implementation of particular actions and solutions that are crucial elements of the proposed practice. Due to the fact that the aim and guidelines of the proposed practice are not contradictory to national/local policies (or other strategic documents), there are no formal barriers for the implementation of the concept.

Organizational conditions of the implementation

Both Partners agreed that the necessity of making a complex formal application for external funding of such an initiative discourages potentially interested bodies/organizations/ businesses from doing so. One of the Partners was afraid that some additional permissions by institutions should be required. Unfortunately, the Partners had an extremely different opinion about local authorities, institutions and other organizations. Especially the opinions concerning the interest, experience, skills and offered support in the potential practice implementation differed substantially. The Partner operate in highly differing regions, so their evaluations might be distinct.

Financial conditions of the implementation

The difference between the Partners' opinions concerning the access to information and external sources of financing that kind of project was noticed. It might be caused by the regional position (as was mentioned above)..

Is it possible to implement the initiative in Poland? – needed support, threats and benefits

The risk of failure of proposed practice implementation was estimated as low by both Partners.

One of the crucial factors determining the success of every initiative is motivation (of the senior employees and the employers) to improve skills. It is necessary to take some activities/ promote the necessity of lifelong learning. They was started a few years ago, so it should be developed and continued.

At the beginning, a skill map should be prepared on the strategic level (national and/or local), allowing the educational and training institutions to draw up a proper programme.

Conditions of potential transfer of best practices from Sweden to Lithuania

The necessity of implementation

In Lithuanian public and private business sectors it is very popular to send the employees to raise their qualifications in conferences, trainings or seminars of varied kinds.

CEDEFOP [http://www.cedefop.europa.eu/EN/Index.aspx] data shows that in Lithuania:

— fewer adults are involved in lifelong learning than the EU as a whole (4.0% and 9.1% respectively), which is below the average target (15%) set by the strategic framework of education and training 2020.

The Lithuanian project Partner, the PP5 VPU Lithuanian University of Educational Sciences, did not point to any solution similar to presented practice.

In Lithuania one of the lowest rates of adult participation in continuous learning in BSR countries is observed, similar to the one present in Poland and Latvia. (see: **Introduction**) Among the seniors (individuals aged 55 and more), this rate is below 10%.

Legal conditions of the implementation

No regulations that could hinder the implementation process were identified in Lithuania. The existing regulations are flexible enough and thus allow for the implementation of particular actions and solutions that are crucial elements of this practice. The aim and guidelines of the proposed practice is not contradictory to Lithuanian national/local policies (and other strategic documents).

Organizational conditions of the implementation

In Lithuania the local government/institutions/partners will probably be interested in implementing this kind of practice. The institutions have sufficient experience, skills and competences necessary for implementing the initiatives like the proposed one and can offer necessary support for other bodies. Improving or obtaining skills is still popular in Lithuania, so potential beneficiaries of such practice would display sufficient motivation to participate in it.

Financial conditions of the implementation

The potential barrier for the implementation of the practice could be the lack of information about external (i.e. public or private) sources of financing this kind of initiative. However, Lithuanian institutions potentially interested in implementing the practice could probably use their own founds to finance it. In the Partner's opinion, this practice would rather not require EU funding or special permission.

Is it possible to implement the initiative in Lithuania? – needed support, threats and benefits

The risk of failure of the proposed practice was evaluated as low. However, the implementation requires full engagement and collaboration of different bodies and organizations across the whole country.

In Lithuania the employers accept the improving of employee qualifications. A ranking of companies enabling their workers to raise their qualifications at company, not only work, is prepared.

The main activity is related to mapping future skills (according to the market needs) and preparing a suitable programme, the way of financing/ co-financing by the participants etc.

Conditions of potential transfer of best practices from Sweden to Latvia

The necessity of implementation

The Latvian Partner, the State Education Centre (VISC), gave an example a solution similar to the proposed one: courses within the framework of the "How to become an entrepreneur in 5 days" programme were organized by higher education institutions financially supported by the Latvian Agency of Development.

According to the Eurostat data, one of the lowest rates of adult participation in continuous learning in BSR countries is observed in Latvia, similar to the one present in Poland and Lithuania. (see: Introduction).

CEDEFOP [http://www.cedefop.europa.eu/EN/Index.aspx] data shows that in Latvia:

— fewer adults are involved in lifelong learning than the EU as a whole (5.0% and 9.1% respectively) and from 2005 to 2010 this share has been falling
— rates of participation of the older and unemployed adults are low in comparison with the EU average.

These are the arguments for attempting at the adaptation and implementation of the proposed practice.

Legal conditions of the implementation

There are no regulations in Latvia which allow for implementation of this project. Moreover, the existing regulations are not flexible enough, so undertaking this practice and implementing its crucial elements would require additional permissions by institutions. The necessity of making a complex formal application for external funding of such an initiative discourages the potentially interested bodies/organizations/businesses from doing so. These activities could be time-consuming, but – according to the fact that the aim and guidelines of the proposed practice are not contradictory to national/local policies and other strategic documents – they might be successful.

Organizational conditions of the implementation

Diversity of similar courses could be a vital obstacle to adaptation and implementation of the practice. In addition, there is no interest among local government/institutions/partners in implementing this kind of practice. These organizations are not well-experienced or skilled, so they could not offer the necessary support for other bodies that would implement this practice. Moreover, this practice is contradictory to traditional way of thinking and acting in Latvia in terms of integration of economically excluded groups into the labour market. At the end, the potential beneficiaries of such practice would not display sufficient motivation to participate in this practice /there are not enough incentives for participating in this practice.

Financial conditions of the implementation

In Latvia there is a limited access to external (public/private) sources for financing this kind of project. In the Partner's opinion, this practice requires applying for EU funding which is not guaranteed.

Is it possible to implement the initiative in Latvia? – needed support, threats and benefits

The crucial is the answer to the question if the institutions potentially interested in implementing this kind of solution dispose own founds which allow for the implementation of the initiative. Due to the fact that the risk of failure was evaluated as high, many activities should be undertaken to prevent it, for example:

— the promotion of results/ impact achieved after delivering such training on individual basis,
— training for parties interested in delivery such a program,
— the crucial activity for success of implementation is to encourage the institutions/ local authorities for implementing the practice showing the benefit,
— for economy (e. g. higher employment rate),
— for society (e.g. inclusion policy),
— for individuals (e. g. well-being).

In the Partner' opinion this practice doesn't require full engagement and collaboration of different bodies and organizations across the whole country.

Summary

The best practices chosen for the transfer and implementation in the Baltic Sea Region from Norway, Sweden, Finland and other countries to Pomerania, North Germany, Lithuania, Latvia and Poland as part of the IGA Quick project are, among other aims, supposed to enhance the existing awareness and knowledge on the potential work to be done in the area of women and elderly involvement in the present and future job market in Baltic Sea Region. This implementation is meant to take place among individuals, enterprises, associations such as chambers for SMEs, public bodies such as local governments. Also, best practices can become subject of promotion by local and national media. Therefore, the purpose of the dissemination of the practices has many dimensions. Combating and changing the stereotypes about the role of the older people and women in economy, labour market are one of them. The very promotion of these can serve as an effective tool for transforming cultural attitudes that are very often neglected in public discourse on labour and social policies.

As it can be seen, the presented examples direct the issue of higher women and elderly participation in the labour market but more specifically are aimed to promote women in management positions, promote their entrepreneurship, support equal remuneration for work.

Without doubt, there are some challenges in the implementation of best practices. As mentioned in Part II of the work, there needs to be commonness of purpose between the good practice and organization implementing it. Competences in the organization should fit the requirements of the practice and organization members should know and understand the principles of a practice. Also, the team of people responsible for transfer should be properly selected. On the managerial side there should be efforts directed to building conducive environment, commitment and openness to feedback on how the practice is absorbed by the organization.

In their evaluation of barriers and stimulants for the practice transfer and implementation on the external side, the partners acknowledge lack of own resources among potentially interested organizations and also limited external sources for financing such undertakings. At the same time they agree that elderly activity on the professional level and women involvement in the labour market is regarded as a problem. On the institutional level, partners do not support the opinion that there are not sufficient regulations and these are not flexible so that the practices should be implemented. Yet, on the informal institutional level, presented practices do not seem to pose a challenge that would create contradictory actions towards traditional ways of thinking. So, despite the lack of potential resource base for initiating such practices, the assessment of conditions for the transfer and implementation is quite positive. Also partners see the potential place for implementation of the proposed good practices. Although some readers of this work may find similar undertakings in countries for the transfer such as Germany, Poland, Lithuania, Latvia, our respondent Partners see the need for further and wider transfer and implementation. Also, as the reader may have observed, some of these practices such as Women Ambassadors in Entrepreneurship are already implemented in the potentially interested regions and countries.

Surely, the undertaken research and analysis, can work as partial view of the reality and opportunities for implementation. The Partners - stakeholders involved in the survey expressed their subjective opinions and in some cases expressed diverse views on the transfer and implementation potential. But as discussed earlier, there seems to be common agreement on overall transfer and implementation potential. This evaluation was particularly difficult for some Partners regarding institutional environment, and legal framework in particular. Nevertheless, there is a common attitude that there is a need and capacity for using the outlined practices as exemplary actions for building more innovative economy in Baltic Sea Region with the higher participation of women and the elderly in the job market in many forms. This is particularly important in the face of existing and forthcoming socio-demographic challenges of Europe.

The authors present the practices so that they could be emulated and modified according to the needs and conditions for transfer and adaptation in local contexts and individual countries. The implementation finally depends on the level of interest and involvement of interested parties. This work has a strong practical angle and so includes relevant referencing and contact details for interested parties.

References

1. *A strategy for smart, sustainable and inclusive growth EUROPE 2020* (2010) Communication from the Commission COM(2010) 2020 final, Brussels.
2. *Ageing in the Twenty-First Century: A Celebration and A Challenge* (2012) United Nations Population Fund (UNFPA), New York.
3. Bielecka M. (2011) *Partnerstwo terytorialne dla rozwoju regionalnego i lokalnego*, Barometr Regionalny 4(26)/2011.
4. Bogan C.E. and English M.J. (1994). *Benchmarking for Best Practices: Winning Through Innovative* Adaptation. New York: McGraw-Hill.
5. Employment Observatory Review, 2010, http://www.eu-employment-observatory.net/
6. *Europa 2020*, http://ec.europa.eu/europe2020/europe-2020-in-a-nutshell/priorities/index_en.htm
7. Eurostat, 2010, http://epp.eurostat.ec.europa.eu/portal/page/portal/eurostat/home/
8. Eurostat, 2011, http://epp.eurostat.ec.europa.eu/portal/page/portal/eurostat/home/
9. Eurostat, 2012, http://epp.eurostat.ec.europa.eu/portal/page/portal/eurostat/home/
10. Grzesiak M., Olczyk M., Richert-Kaźmierska A., Starnawska M. (2013), *The best practices transfer part II*, Report produced within Work Package 4 of the EU-funded project QUICK IGA
11. Grzesiak M., Olczyk M., Starnawska M. (2013), *The best practices transfer part I*, Report produced within Work Package 4 of the EU-funded project QUICK IGA
12. Grzesiak M., Richert-Kaźmierska A. (2013), *The analysis of the conditions for best practices' transfer*, Report produced within Work Package 4 of the EU-funded project QUICK IGA
13. http://www.themanagementor.com/kuniverse/kmailers_universe/manu_k mailers/bp_ensurecomp3.htm [24.06.2013]
14. Kaczmarek B., Cz. Sikorski, Podstawy zarządzania. Zachowania organizacyjne, Absolwent, Łódź 1998, p. 24.
15. Karwińska A., Wiktor D. (2008), *Przedsiębiorczość i korzyści społeczne: identyfikacja dobrych praktyk w ekonomii*, Ekonomia społeczna, No 6.
16. Kautonen T. (2008) *Understanding the older entrepreneur: Comparing Third Age and Prime Age entrepreneurs in Finland*, "Int. Journal of Business Science and Applied Management", Volume 3, Issue 3.

17. Kautonen T. (2013) *Senior entrepreneurship*, A background paper for the OECD Centre for Entrepreneurship, SMEs and Local Development, Turku.

18. Konopacka A. (2011) *Podręcznik antydyskryminacyjny*, Wessling Polska, Kraków.

19. *Kształcenie dorosłych* (2009) GUS, Warszawa.

20. Nash J. and Ehrenfeld, J., 1997: Codes of environmental management practice: assessing their potential as a tool for change. Annual Review of Energy and the Environment 22.

21. *Political Declaration and Madrid International Plan of Action on Ageing* (2002) Second World Assembly on Ageing, Madrid 8-12.04.2002, http://undesadspd.org/Portals/0/ageing/documents/Fulltext-E.pdf (10.02.2014).

22. Stabryła A., J. Trzcieniecki, Organizacja i zarządzanie. Zarys problematyki, Akademia Ekonomiczna w Krakowie, Kraków 1986, p. 183–184.

23. Szukalski P. (red.) (2008) *To idzie starość – polityka społeczna a przygotowanie do starzenia się ludności Polski*, Instytut Spraw Publicznych, Warszawa.

24. Tivig T., Frosch K., Kühntopf S. (2008) *Mapping Regional Demographic Change and Regional Demographic Location Risk in Europe*, Final Report, Rostock.

25. *World Population Ageing 2013* (2013) Department of Economic and Social Affairs Population Division, United Nations New York.

26. Zeytinoglu I.U. (ed.) (2005) *Flexibility in Workplaces: Effects on Workers*, Work Environment and the Unions, Geneva.

27. US Department of Commerce (2010), *Women-Owned Businesses in the 21st Century*, prepared by the US Department of Commerce, Economics and Statistics Administration for the White House Council on Women and Girls.

Annex I – Questionnaire

Dear Sir/Madame,

This evaluation sheet is used for the purpose of the IGA QUICK Project. It is used for the analysis and evaluation of transfer potential of the particular practice into your country/region. The analysis of gathered answers will let us provide important recommendations for future transfer of these practices. Beneath you will find questions where we ask you to mark "x" in chosen answer. We would greatly appreciate your feedback. Thank you in advance.

In the table below you will find statements regarding the potential for transfer and implementation of the discussed practice (we call it "best practice"). These statements refer to economic, legal, social and organizational issues in assessment of implementation potential. We kindly ask you to insert "x" depending whether you definitely agree with the statement, rather agree/disagree with the statement, have no opinion, disagree with the statement.

Partner No……………….   **Best Practice No**

	Definitely agree	Rather agree	I have no opinion	Rather disagree	Definitely disagree
In our country/region there are no or very little own sources among institutions potentially interested in implementing this kind of solution.					
In our country/region there is a limited access to external (public/private) sources for financing this kind of project.					
In our country/region there is a limited access to information about potential external financial sources for this kind of project.					
This practice requires applying for EU funding which is not guaranteed.					
In our country/region there are no regulations that					

allow for implementation of this project.					
In our country/region the regulations are not flexible enough and so do not allow to take into account particular actions and solutions that are a crucial element of this practice.					
Undertaking this practice requires additional permissions etc. by institutions implementing it.					
The aim and guidelines of the proposed practice is contradictory with national/local policies (and so strategic documents).					
The necessity of making a complex formal application for external funding of such an initiative discourages potentially interested bodies/organizations/businesses to do so.					
In our country/region there is no interest among local government/institutions/partners in implementing this kind of practice.					
In our country/region local government/institutions/partners do not have sufficient experience, skills and competences necessary for implementing this kind of practice.					
In our country/region local government/institutions/partners cannot offer necessary support for other bodies that would implement this practice.					
This practice is contradictory to traditional way of thinking and acting in our country/region in terms of integration of economically excluded groups into the labour market.					
In our country/region potential beneficiaries of such practice would not display sufficient motivation to participate in this practice /there are not enough incentives for participating in this practice.					

In our country/region innovation level is not regarded as a problem.					
In our country/region low economic activity of women is not regarded as a problem.					
In our country/region low economic activity of the elderly is not regarded as a problem.					
In our country/region there are already similar practices like this one and there is no need to implement this one.					
This practice requires full engagement and collaboration of different bodies and organizations across the whole country.					
The risk of failure for this practice is high.					

Please provide similar projects or practices in case such were run in your country.

....
....
....
....
....
....
....
....

Please suggest what activities could raise more interest in the proposed initiative.

....
....
....
....

....
....

....
....

Please suggest what kind of support would be required in case of implementation of such initiative.

....
....

....
....

....
....

....
....

Annex II – The best practices catalogue cards

Female future mobilizing talents –a business perspective

Title of initiative	FEMALE FUTURE – MOBILIZING TALENTS -A BUSINESS PERSPECTIVE		
Category	Education/Training	**Country**	Norway
leader of the initiative	**Confederation of Norwegian Enterprise** (NHO)		
Target group	talented women working in private enterprises		
Characteristics of the initiative	The aim of the project is to bring more women into top management positions as well as into the companies' boardrooms.		
Results	62% of the participants were offered board positions or advanced in their management career.		
For further information	http://www.nho.no/ff/		
Contact	**NHO – Confederation of Norwegian Enterprise** Kari Maeland P.O.Box 5250 Majorstuen N-0303 Oslo Email: firmapost@nho.no Phone: + 47 23 08 80 00 Fax: + 47 23 08 80 01		

Women into technology

Title of initiative	Women into Technology (WIT)		
Category	Employment support	**Country**	Scoltand
leader of the initiative	**Fife Women's Technology Centres**		
Target group	Women (18+) with low or no previous qualifications, who have been out of the labour market for long periods.		
For further information	http://www.fwtc.net/		
Contact	Fife Women's Technology Centre Lohgelly Miner's Institute 129 Main Street, Lochgelly KY5 9AF, UK +44159784847		

Fuuturi: Women entrepreneurs and managers in the future

Title of initiative	Fuuturi: Women entrepreneurs and managers in the future		
Category	Women entrepreneurship support	**Country**	Finland
Leader of the initiative	Ylä-Savo Municipal Federation of Education		
Target group	Women entrepreneurs in existing business or women managers and employees		
For further information	http://www.rakennerahastot.fi/rakennerahastot/tiedostot/hyvaeae_hanketoimintaa_EN/yrittjyys_tasa-arvo_Futuuri_ENG_lores.pdf http://www.ysao.fi/Suomeksi/Kehittamispalvelut/Paattyneet_hankkeet/Futuuri.iw3 http://www.futuuri-projekti.fi/ (initiative website no longer working)		
Contact	Kari Puumalainen, kari.puumalainen@ysao.fi Ylä-Savon koulutuskuntayhtymä / Ylä-Savon ammattiopisto Asevelikatu 4, 74100 Iisalmi + 358 400 793 155		

Pay Equity Action Plan

Title of initiative	Pay Equity Action Plan		
Category	Government policy/	**Country**	Sweden
leader of the initiative	Equal Opportunities Ombudsman (JamO)		
Target group	All enterprises/ organizations with more than 10 employees		
For further information	http://www.do.se		
Contact	DO Box 3686 103 59 Stockholm Sweden +46 (0)8 120 20 700		

Women@Work

Title of initiative	Women@Work (W@W)		
Category	skill development	**Country**	United Kingdom
Leader of the initiative	Workers Educational Association		
Target group	Employed women who have job experience		
For further information	http://www.weawomenatwork.org.uk/about		
Contact	Cath Findlay +44 1463 710577 WEA David Whyte House 57 Church Street Inverness IV1 1DR		

Ambassadors for Women's entrepreneurship

Title of initiative	Ambassadors for Women's entrepreneurship		
Category	Promotion of women entrepreneurship	Country	Sweden
Leader of the initiative	Swedish Agency for Economic and Regional Growth		
Target group	Young women Pupils at schools, students at universities Broader audience: All possible stakeholders –in the society and economy.		
For further information	www.ambassadorer.se		
Contact	Carin Persson Projektledare + 46 8681 91 46 carin.persson@tillvaxtverket.se Swedish Agency for Economic and Regional Growth Box 4044 SE-102 61 Stockholm Sweden		

Senior policy in working life

Title of initiative	Senior policy in working life		
Category	Socio-economic policy	**Country**	Norway
Leader of the initiative	Center for Senior Policy (CSP)		
Target group	workers from the age of 45-50		
Characteristics of the initiative	The aim of this initiative is to keep the elders as long as possible in labour market.		
Results	http://www.vinnvinn.org/employees.99573.en.html http://www.vinnvinn.org/representatives.99574.en.html http://www.vinnvinn.org/employers.99572.en.html		
For further information	http://www.seniorpolitikk.no/informasjon/english		
Contact	Senter for seniorpolitikk St Olavs plass 3 0165 Oslo, Norway Phone: 0047 23 15 65 50 E-mail:ssp@seniorpolitikk.no		

Senior enterprises – experience never ages

Title of initiative	Senior enterprises – experience never ages		
Category	Entrepreneurship	**Country**	Ireland
Leader of the initiative	The Mid East Regional Authority		
Target group	Persons aged 50+: employees, unemployed, economically inactive		
For further information	http://www.seniorenterprise.ie		
Contact	Senior Enterprise, The Mid East Regional Authority, County Buildings, Wicklow Town, Co.Wicklow, Ireland. Tel: +353 (0) 404 66058 Email: info@seniorenterprise.ie		

Flexible work practices

Title of initiative	Flexible work practices		
Category	Age management	**Country**	Sweden
Leader of the initiative	Kronoberg County Council		
Target group	Employees aged 55+		
For further information	Carl Krekola, Personnel manager, email: carl.krekola@ltkronoberg.se		
Contact	Landstinget Kronoberg, 351 88 Växjö Telephone 0470-58 80 00 landstinget@ltkronoberg.se		

Higher Vocational Education

Title of initiative	Higher Vocational Education		
Category	Education	**Country**	Sweden
Leader of the initiative	Sensus Study Association		
Target group	Adults (35+) interested in upgrading their skills (average age of Sensus' students – 38 years old)		
For further information	http://www.sensus.se/Hjalpsidor1/Alla-sprak/EngelskaOmSensus/		
Contact	Sensus studieförbund Box 11003 404 21 Göteborg Kursanmälan: 031-708 39 50 Växel: 031-708 39 00 Fax: 031-708 39 99 E-post: goteborg@sensus.se		

Publications of the Baltic Sea Academy

Volume 1
Strategies for the Development of Crafts and SMEs
in the Baltic Sea Region
2011
ISBN: 9783842326125

Volume 2
Strategy Programme for education policies in the Baltic Sea Region
2012 (2nd edition)
ISBN: 9783848252534

Volume 3
Education Policy Strategies today and tomorrow around the "Mare Balticum"
2011
IBSN: 9783842374218

Volume 4
Energy Efficiency and Climate Protection around the
Mare Balticum
2011
ISBN: 9783844800982

Volume 5
SME relevant sectors in the BSR: Personnel organisation, Energy and
Construction
2012
ISBN: 9783848202577

Volume 6
Strategies and Promotion of Innovation in Regional Policies around the Mare
Balticum
2012
IBSN 9783848218295

Volume 7
Strategy Programme for innovation in regional policies in the Baltic Sea
Region
2012
ISBN: 9783848230471

Volume 8
Humanivity - Innovative economic development through human growth by
Kenneth Daun
2012
ISBN: 9783848253395

Volume 9
Economic Perspectives, Qualification and Labour Market Integration of
Women in the Baltic Sea Region
2013
ISBN: 9783732243952

Volume 10
Corporate Social Responsebility and Women's Entrepreneurship around the
Mare Balticum
2013
ISBN: 9783732278459

Volume 11
Development of the enterprises' competitiveness in the context of
demographic challenges
2013
ISBN: 973732293971

Volume 12
Age, Gender and Innovation – Strategy program and action plans for the
Baltic Sea Region
2014
ISBN: 9783735784919

Volume 13
Innovative SMEs by Gender and Age around the Mare Balticum
2014
ISBN: 9783735791191

Volume 14
Innovation in SMEs, previous projects in the Baltic Sea Region and future needs
2014
ISBN: 9783735791191

Volume 15
Building the socially responsible employment policy in the Baltic Sea Region
2014
ISBN: 9783735790484

Volume 16
Women and elderly on the BSR labour market - good practices' analysis and transfer
2014
ISBN: 9783735791412

Members of the Hanse-Parlament

The Chamber of Craftmanship and Enterprise in Białystok

Brest Department of the Belarusian Chamber of Commerce and Industry

Hungarian Association of Craftsmen Corporations

Företagarna Kalmar länCottbus Chamber of Skilled Crafts and SME's

Dresden Chamber of Skilled Crafts and Small Businesses

Pomeranian Chamber of Handicrafts for SME's

Hamburg Chamber of Skilled Crafts and Small Businesses

The Federation of Finnish Enterprises

Chamber of Craft Region Kaliningrad

Kaliningrad Regional Economic Development Agency

Chamber of Crafts and SME in Katowice

Chamber of Crafts and SME in Kielce

Handicraft Chamber of Ukraine

Handicraft Chamber Leningrad Region

The Craft Chamber of Łódź

Företagarna Skåne Service AB

Belarusian Chamber of Commerce and Industry

Minsk Department of the Belarussian Chamber of Commerce and Industry

Mogilev Branch of Belarusian Chamber of Commerce and Industry

Russian Chamber of Crafts

Warmia and Mazury Chamber of Crafts and Small Business in Olsztyn

Chamber of Crafts in Opole

The Norwegian Federation of Craft Enterprises

Master of Crafts Norway

Eastern Mecklenburg-Western Pomerania Chamber of Handicraft

Panevėžys Chamber of Commerce, Industry and Crafts

Satakunnan Yrittajät R.Y.

Wielkopolska Craft Chamber in Poznań

Latvian Chamber of Crafts

Craft Chamber in Rzeszów

Schwerin Chamber of Skilled Crafts

The Chamber of Handicraft Middle Pomerania in Słupsk
The St. Petersburg Crafts Chamber
The Chamber of Crafts and SME in Szczecin
Estonian Association of Small and Medium Enterprises
The Baltic Institute of Finland
The Organisation of Handicraft Businesses in Trondheim
Vilnius Chamber of Commerce, Industry and Crafts
Lithuanian Business Employers Confederation
The Chamber of Crafts of Mazovia, Kurpie and Podlasie Regions in Warsaw
Small Business Chamber Warsaw
The Lower Silesian Chamber of Craft and Small and Medium-sized Businesses
Kyiv Chamber of Commerce and Industry
IBC Innovationsfabrikken Kolding
Donskaya Craft Chamber in Rostov/Don
Nordic Forum of Crafts

Members of the Baltic Sea Academy

Brest State Technical University, Belarus

University 21 non-profit limited Liability Company, Germany

Hamburg University of Corporate Education, Germany

Hamburg Institute of International Economics, Germany

Hanse-Parlament e.V., Germany

International Business Academy, Denmark

Lund University, Sweden

Satakunta University of Applied Sciences, Finland

University of Latvia, Latvia

Gdansk University of Technology, Poland

Panevėžys College

Hanseatic Academy of Management, Słupsk, Poland

Saint-Petersburg State University of Economics, Russia

Tampere University of Technology, Finland

Vilnius Gediminas Technical University, Lithuania

Vilnius Pedagogical University, Lithuania

University of Bialystok, Poland

Võru County Vacational Training Centre, Estonia